GATLAND'S LAST BOW

Wales in Japan, 2019

"The biggest thing I'm proud of is that we've earned respect from the rest of the world… I'm not sure that was there before."

WARREN GATLAND

"Before Warren, Welsh rugby didn't have the confidence to say 'We expect to win.' But now we go into games with confidence."

JONATHAN DAVIES

GATLAND'S LAST BOW

Wales in Japan, 2019

Richard Morgan

For Katja

First impression: 2019

© Copyright Richard Morgan and Y Lolfa Cyf., 2019

The contents of this book are subject to copyright, and may
not be reproduced by any means, mechanical or electronic,
without the prior, written consent of the publishers.

The publishers wish to acknowledge the support of
the Books Council of Wales

Cover images: PA Images
Cover design: Y Lolfa

All images from the author's own collection
unless otherwise stated

ISBN: 978 1 912631 25 4

Published and printed in Wales
on paper from well-maintained forests by
Y Lolfa Cyf., Talybont, Ceredigion SY24 5HE
website www.ylolfa.com
e-mail ylolfa@ylolfa.com
tel 01970 832 304
fax 832 782

Contents

七転び八起き

Fall down seven times but stand up eight.

JAPANESE PROVERB

Acknowledgements

FIRST AND FOREMOST, I'd like to thank Tom Brown-Lowe and Siân Thomas, my ITV Wales colleagues, who were such a pleasure to work with in Japan. Without them, it would have been difficult to find the material to fill this book! Thanks also to my editor, Carolyn Hodges, for the constant supply of support and good ideas, and to Lefi Gruffudd at Y Lolfa, for agreeing to take on the project in the first place. Finally, thanks to all those – Welsh, Japanese and other nationalities – who agreed to be interviewed by ITV (and by extension, for this book). I couldn't have done it without you.

Richard Morgan
November 2019

Foreword

HAVING LIVED IN Japan myself, it didn't surprise me to see how well the Japanese people looked after fans at Rugby World Cup 2019.

Everyone I spoke to said how friendly and accommodating the people were, despite the language barrier. And I believe the good spirit around the tournament was one reason we saw so much magnificent rugby.

Wales did particularly well. The comeback wins against Fiji and France showed how much the World Cup meant to them. You're always going to get injuries in a long tournament, and by the end it felt like last man standing. The fact that Jonathan Davies and Rhys Patchell, both since ruled out for long spells with injury, played until the last game says it all about the commitment. In the end, though, it was a couple of games too far for Wales, who lost to eventual champions South Africa.

But I believe we're going to get better. The system Warren Gatland has put in place will stand us in good stead. Now we have new coaches coming in, with fresh ideas about how they want Wales to play. Defensively, Wales have been one of the best teams in the world for the past five or six years. But we can improve with ball in hand, and I think Wayne Pivac and

Stephen Jones can make that happen. With lots of youngsters coming through, and plenty of experience, we're in a good position. Now it's about building for the next World Cup, and being even more prepared.

As a whole, World Rugby is getting more competitive. This tournament saw the so-called Tier 2 sides give a great account of themselves. And Japan's performances have arguably earned them the right to enter a higher-level tournament, like the Rugby Championship or Six Nations. As fans, we want other teams to develop, be more competitive, and help rugby grow. Hopefully, in future, we'll see the World Cup played in more countries where rugby's not the number 1 sport.

If you were lucky enough to be there, I hope this book brings back happy memories of Japan. If you weren't, I hope it gives you an idea of what it was like.

Arigatō.

Shane Williams
November 2019

Prologue

27 October: 19:46

There are 75 minutes on the clock, and it's sort of appropriate that the fate of Wales' World Cup campaign should come down to this: a shot at goal by South Africa's Handré Pollard. For the past hour and a quarter of play, this has, after all, been a game defined by kicking. Not just the 22 points landed from the tee, but the endless, mind-numbing tactical punts exchanged by Gareth Davies and Faf de Klerk. It's been a test of patience even for the stoic Japanese spectators, who, as usual, have helped swell the crowd here at Yokohama Stadium. And now, after Dillon Lewis or Rhys Carré – I'm not sure which – was penalised for doing something he shouldn't have at a maul, Pollard is readying himself to put boot to leather once again. After nearly 480 minutes of rugby and seven weeks of criss-crossing the islands of Japan, Wales' fate at Rugby World Cup 2019 is about to be decided.

It's been an odyssey, and ideally it will end next Saturday, back here in Yokohama, with the legendary Alun Wyn Jones holding aloft the Webb Ellis Cup. But if Alun Wyn and his troops can't conquer the world, they've at least made it sit up and take notice.

"The biggest thing I'm proud of is that we've earned respect from the rest of the world for what we've achieved," said Warren Gatland, Wales' outgoing coach, this week. "I'm not sure that was there before that."

It wasn't, as I'm sure Warren knows. A little over 12 years ago, I was half a world away in France, watching the final throes of another World Cup adventure. It was a lot more entertaining than this one, for sure, with two teams throwing the ball around for fun in the autumn sunshine. But no amount of champagne skills could sweeten the pill for Wales when they lost to Fiji in Nantes, and forfeited their place in the quarter-finals. The next day, coach Gareth Jenkins was ignominiously sacked in a hotel car park and World Rugby's rankings showed Wales in 10th place. 'Respect' and 'Welsh rugby' were not words you'd have heard uttered in the same sentence.

It's different these days. Now Wales are a team to get Springbok great Bryan Habana shifting nervously in his seat as he tries to predict the outcome of the game in a pre-match interview. They're a team who have beaten England twice this year, and who would fancy their chances of making it three, should they play them again in next week's final. A team with real belief, inspired by a record run of wins and a track record of exceeding expectations.

Granted, it's not always pretty. Wales rarely tear teams apart with attacking brilliance. Rather, they suffocate them slowly through attrition and a tireless appetite for tackling. They're a sort of rugby boa constrictor. A collection of honest workhorses with a few thoroughbreds thrown in. In sporting parlance, they've 'forgotten how to lose'. Against Fiji and France in this tournament, they looked down and out but bounced back off the canvas. Even tonight, Damian de Allende's try might have broken their resolve. But from a penalty, Wales had the guts to take on the Springbok scrum, and scored a converted try of their own. They're nothing if not tough.

But even these arch-escapologists are running out of road now. Pollard swings his boot and the assistant referees raise their flags. 19-16. Moments later, Alun Wyn – of all people – drops the ball at a line-out and the 'Boks have a scrum. There are 2 minutes left. Even if Wales can somehow regain the ball, they'll have to get themselves down the other end of the field against the world's most miserly defence. I exchange glances with Tom and Siân, my ITV News colleagues and constant companions over the past crazy month and a half.

Is this the end of the world?

1

31 men

2 September: The Class of '19

Eight weeks earlier. A fresh, early autumn morning at the National Centre of Excellence, known simply as 'the Barn' to those who use it. This is the setting for the official unveiling of Wales' Rugby World Cup squad – the 31 men selected to carry the hopes of the nation to Japan later in the month.

'The Barn' – a large, warehouse-shaped building at the far end of the Vale of Glamorgan Hotel car park – is the place where Wales do their hard yards. Where bodies are flayed into shape, the better to withstand the white heat of international rugby. At its centre is a large artificial pitch. Today, scattered across the synthetic grass, divided into written and broadcast 'pods', are the great Welsh rugby media, ready to feast on the 30-odd blokes in whom a nation will be investing its dreams.

It's 14 weeks since they first gathered, in an extended training squad of 42, back in June. Since then, their lives have been a study in sweat. Sweat on the pitch; sweat in the gym; sweat in Switzerland, where they spent a gruelling week at altitude, sleeping 'high' and training 'low', the better to optimise their bodies' use of oxygen; sweat at the 'heat stress' camp in Turkey, designed to prepare them for humid Japan.

At last, in August, a release, of sorts, with three 'warm-up' matches: England, away and home, and Ireland... the chance to audition in front of the watching Wales coaches, as if on some particularly painful TV talent show.

And this morning, we meet these survivors of that hellish boot camp: 31 chiselled, toughened men. 1,066 caps between them, aged from 21 at the youngest to a venerable 33. Milling about uncomfortably on the artificial turf waiting for us reporters to approach them, like speed-daters who wished they'd stayed at home.

Here's James Davies, brother of Wales centre Jonathan. Davies the elder is now on 75 caps; for the younger sibling, a foraging flanker from the Scarlets, it's been an altogether harder road to international recognition. But, after years in the wilderness and a number of recent injury setbacks, his big breakthrough has come: yesterday – selection day – and zero hour of 2 o'clock came and went... with no rejection message.

"It was an hour when you were just waiting for the text of death. But I managed to get to 2 o'clock and I didn't have it."

It means the man known as 'Cubby Boi' will be able to add a World Cup campaign to his Olympic Sevens adventure in Rio in 2016. And, what's more, he'll do it alongside his brother, an established Wales star named 'Man of the Series' for the Lions two years ago.

"It's great to see two of us going over there. Mum and Dad were already going because 'Golden-Balls' was. So now they get two for the price of one!"

14

"I remember saying to Gatland a few weeks ago, 'If I was left out of this back row, I'd have no qualms about it.' Everyone's world class. For them to put me in… it's great."

Ross Moriarty, also named among the back rows, has his own family connection with the World Cup. His dad, Paul, and uncle, Richard, both played at the inaugural tournament, way back in 1987. Richard, in fact, remains Wales' highest-achieving skipper to date on the world stage: he led them to a third-place finish all those years ago.

"My uncle is the best-ranked Wales captain at the World Cup and doesn't get much credit for that. So a shout out to him," Ross smiles. "But we're hoping to do better than that this time…we definitely feel we can do it. Over the last few seasons we've had a lot of new caps and done very well. So we'll definitely be ready to go."

It's a note of optimism that echoes through the morning. And why not? Wales, after all, recently reached the hitherto unscaled summit of World Rugby's rankings, and in doing so knocked the All Blacks off their perch for the first time in ten years. That stint at number 1 may have proved fleeting, but it has left a rare feeling of confidence in the Wales camp… a sense, for once, of real squad depth.

"We've had a few injuries already," says Justin Tipuric, who is a veteran of the 2015 World Cup in England, "and people have stepped up. If we lose one or two, it's not the end of the world, but probably in the past everyone would be like, 'There's no one there to step in.' Now there's a big 30, 40-man squad, where anyone can step on the field and do a great job."

Certainly, the loss to injury of Taulupe Faletau and Gareth Anscombe has been a setback. But with Dan Biggar in reserve at outside half, and a battalion of back-row forwards to cover for Faletau, hope remains.

For Shaun Edwards, Warren Gatland's loyal lieutenant, here since the start of the New Zealander's reign in 2008, this third and final tilt at the Webb Ellis Cup offers a chance to settle unfinished business.

"I've looked enviously on at the last two finals. I'd very much like to be there for the final and take it from there. But that's going to be very difficult. There's great opposition, there's fantastic teams around the world and great coaches. But we're in there with a fighting chance. There doesn't seem to be quite the gulf there was maybe ten years ago between the southern hemisphere teams and the northern hemisphere teams."

If Wales have closed that gap, it is largely due to the defensive solidity instilled by the northerner. The recent Grand Slam campaign saw them concede a miserly 65 points in five games. But Edwards has also spotted a troubling trend: armed with new guidelines from World Rugby, referees are more likely than ever to crack down on tackles that are less than textbook. This summer, reduced to 14 men after the dismissal of Scott Barrett, even the almighty All Blacks went down to a record defeat – 47-26 to Australia.

"Everybody has to make sure their tackle technique is right. Because the way the game is at the moment, anyone can be sent off in the first ten, fifteen minutes. And even if you're heavily fancied to win, if you've only got 14 players on the pitch, that makes it a lot more difficult. I do feel that keeping 15 players on the pitch at all times is going to be massive as regards trying to win the World Cup."

It is a scenario Shaun can imagine all too well. After all, he was sitting in the coach's box on that fateful night at Eden Park back in 2011 when Sam Warburton was given his marching orders for a mistimed tackle on France's Vincent Clerc. That probably cost Wales a World Cup Final appearance; no one would want a repeat.

An unlucky few won't get the chance to try. Props Rob Evans – a Grand Slam-winner as recently as March – and Samson Lee, plus centre Scott Williams, are all big-name omissions from the squad. Lock Cory Hill is included, but is likely to be unavailable until later with a fractured leg. But if, as one ex-player said, one measures a group's abilities by the stature of the players not in it, the class of '19 certainly seems one of the better vintages sent to do battle on the world stage.

Alun Wyn Jones should know. Just shy of his 34th birthday and already on a colossal 127 Wales appearances, the skipper can look at his young charges from the perspective of someone who has survived three previous campaigns... starting with the ill-fated French World Cup of 2007, where Wales were unceremoniously dumped out by Fiji.

"I've had a bit of a mix, really. '07 wasn't the best, going out in the pool stages. '11 we got to the semi-final. We played against Australia in '15 and couldn't capitalise on them having two men yellow-carded. So it's been a bit of a smorgasbord of experiences from my point of view. I do feel a bit of unfinished business with the competition."

Unfinished business – those words again. But is the 2019 squad the one to right the wrongs of campaigns past?

"Well, the jury's out on that. But from a balance, age profile and experience point of view, it's quite exciting. If we fulfil our potential, it becomes even more exciting."

The phoney war is not quite over. On Saturday, Wales will face Ireland again – this time in Dublin – a final hit-out before the serious stuff begins. But today, the tone has changed. Uncertainty has been replaced by relief, and the knowledge that, barring calamity, these 31 will be boarding the plane to Japan in nine days' time.

In just three weeks, some will be running out for the opening match against Georgia in Toyota City.

The World Cup is almost upon us.

2

Tokyo interlude

13 September: First impressions

It's the early hours of Saturday morning – 2.30 a.m. to be specific. But despite the late hour and the early flight tomorrow morning, there'll be no sleep anytime soon. The atmosphere's too electric, my senses too sharpened. I've just done a live broadcast for Wales at Six. We're in the Kabuki-cho district of Tokyo, and the neon lights are like daylight.

Together with ITV colleagues Tom and Siân, I arrived yesterday morning at Tokyo's Narita Airport, more than an hour's train ride from Shinjuku, the area of the city where we're staying. A journey time which gives some sense of the vastness of this place. With 38 million people in the wider metropolitan area, Tokyo is the world's largest city in terms of population. After an afternoon spent sleeping off the jetlag, we venture out for dinner. The streets are thronged with office workers spilling into the night. The hum of cicadas fills the evening air. The wide pavements are pristine, despite the human traffic. Red Chinese lanterns hang outside the bars and restaurants, bobbing gently in the breeze, while far above, the skyscraper windows twinkle. Our Japanese-Italian fusion restaurant provides an interesting introduction to the local cuisine... pasta studded with raw fish, pork and Japanese pickles, washed down with *miso* soup. The description on the English menu is cryptic: 'No. 1 reputation from gentleman – for heavy users.' I'm not sure whether I'm a 'heavy user' of pickles – or a gentleman, for that matter – but it tastes good.

The next day, after picking up our accreditation from Tokyo Stadium, we start filming. At the grandly titled Foreign Correspondents Club of Japan, we meet Ursula Bartlett-Imadegawa, originally from Cardiff, but a Tokyo resident since marrying her Japanese husband. Now she heads the St David's Society, a social club for expats. Feeling like characters from a Graham Greene novel, we sit in the club bar and chat over Darjeeling tea.

"I think the Welsh and the Japanese have a natural affinity. There's a clubbiness, a clannishness, a love of singing. In all areas – technology, food, tourism – the Japanese are fascinated by the beauty of Wales."

She thinks holding the World Cup here will be good for the growth of the game in Japan.

"Rugby's been established in Japan since the nineteenth century, but it was very much a private school game. So there was already a strong foundation of rugby, but it's amazing how the World Cup is spreading it to the local people."

And those people are certainly friendly. The day before, exhausted, I'd collapsed into a taxi minus one of my heavy bags (TV equipment doesn't make for travelling light). Before I knew what was happening, I turned around to find the diminutive female driver happily manhandling the luggage onto the passenger seat.

Courtesy and good manners are ubiquitous. The locals are also, it seems, excited about the looming World Cup, now just a week away. In the official tournament megastore, the fans are full of enthusiasm.

"It's great to have the World Cup in Japan, because it might be an opportunity for people to get to know rugby better," says one. "I hope the Rugby World Cup is good for Japan," says another.

It's an opportunity for Japan, certainly, but also an opportunity for rugby: the first World Cup to be held in Asia, and the chance for the sport to plug into a new market, millions strong. To do that, there's a sense that much will depend on the fortunes of the national team. The 'Brave Blossoms' start their campaign against Russia in seven days' time. One fan from Scotland tells me he'd almost rather see Japan go through from Pool A at his own team's expense, given how home-team involvement in the knockout stages would electrify the nation. Japan's recent Pacific Nations Cup victory gives cause for optimism; last week's 41-7 humbling at the hands of the Springboks less so.

*****

As dusk settles over Tokyo, we're left to ponder the long evening ahead over a late lunch of chicken *katsu*. Japan is eight hours ahead of Wales, which means we won't be on air until 2 a.m. local time. Somewhere across the sprawling city, the Wales squad are acclimatising to life in this different time zone. Tomorrow, they'll fly from here to their training camp on Kyushu, an island in the south of the country. But the 31 men of last week have, for now at least, been reduced to 30. Second row Adam Beard was left behind, stricken with appendicitis, when the squad flew out this week. The WRU say he's had the offending organ removed, and will be fit to link up with the squad 'early next week'. But with Cory Hill also unavailable for the Georgia match, Wales will be short on locks for the start of the tournament.

Wales won't be the only team with injury concerns going into the campaign, of course. England's Mako Vunipola missed his team's final warm-up match with hamstring trouble, while wing Jack Nowell hasn't played all summer, due to a combination of ailments. For Ireland, Keith Earls is a concern, and even New Zealand have picked a player – second row Brodie Retallick – who may be out of contention until the quarter-finals. At least Wales have a winnable game first up; had Australia, not Georgia, been their opening opponents in Pool D, I wonder if they'd have been prepared to risk going into the game with just two fit front-line locks.

All things to ponder as we head out into the bustling night. Downtown, it's a kaleidoscope of neon and sound, with people enjoying their Friday night. We take a lift up to a bar, where I order coffee to keep me alert for the broadcast in a few hours. We're here to meet Sarah Louisa Birchley. Originally from Cwmbran, she moved to Japan 18 years ago to teach English, and is now a professor in business studies at a local university. She's also a member of GlobalWelsh , which aims to promote Wales and its interests around the world.

Over the hubbub, she tells us how the Japanese police have been getting lessons in what to expect from the boisterous rugby fan abroad. Singing in the street, it seems, and sweeping strangers up in a boozy bear-hug, can be alarming in this more reserved culture. But she's also passionate about the opportunity ahead for Wales to build on its historic links with the Land of the Rising Sun:

"Right back as far as the nineteenth century, when Wales sent iron, coal and steel over to Japan to build the railways, there's been a sense of community and family. The geography of the areas is very, very similar. There's something very special about Japan and Wales. There's a connection you can't quite put into words."

She says there'll be a busy programme of events for Welsh business visitors in the build-up to the Australia game.

"There are Welsh companies coming over to watch the games and do some business on the side. It's a huge opportunity for Wales to push its brand and put us up on the global stage so that we can create more opportunities; for jobs back in Wales, and for Welsh people to come to do business in Tokyo."

With Brexit – if it ever happens – on the horizon, it's a heartening thought: the chance for businesses, using rugby as a vehicle, to find new havens of economic opportunity. For them, these uncertain times mean the tournament is about much more than sport.

2 o'clock comes and we do our bit for the news. It feels surreal in the shining lights of Tokyo. Again, we're struck by

the sense of safety, even in this nightlife district. Revellers pass and call out good-humouredly, clearly enjoying their evening. But they're far too polite to interfere with what we're doing. There's no vomit, no fights, and no prone bodies lying in the gutter. It's hard to imagine filming in Cardiff's St Mary Street at this hour without someone mooning, cursing or rugby-tackling one of the crew.

Decompressing over a pint at the Irish bar around the corner, we're left to reflect on a whirlwind first 36 hours in Japan. The World Cup is certainly on the radar, even here in this giant city, and it feels like there's much more to come. There is for us, too: in a few hours we'll be boarding another plane, bound for the southern island of Kyushu, and our first encounter with the Wales team.

3

Kitakyushu –
ups and downs

14 September: Go, Go Wales

From the moment we step out of the plane into the heat
and humidity of southern Japan, to be greeted by an airport
staff member dressed in a Wales jersey, it's clear that we're
in for something special in Kitakyushu. An impression only
increased by the 'Go, Go Wales' posters and the Welsh flags
on the walls above the baggage carousel.

The team arrived an hour before us. The crowds have now
dispersed, but a quick glance at social media gives a sense of
the warmth of their reception. The videos show kids in rugby
jerseys singing the national anthem and clamouring for
autographs, entranced by these giants from a faraway land.

It's the same in town that evening, where the quintessentially
Japanese arcades are festooned with Welsh flags. From the
walls, Alun Wyn Jones and other man-mountains glower
down impressively. Even Kokura Castle is lit up red. City
buses pass by, emblazoned with images of the team.

18 months ago, I imagine very few people in Kitakyushu
had heard of Wales, let alone its rugby players. But when

the city learned it wouldn't be hosting a World Cup game, its leaders invited the WRU to hold a training camp here. And the WRU, to its credit, seized the opportunity. Since then, outreach teams have visited several times to build links with the community, organising rugby classes for children and meeting with businesses and universities.

On today's evidence, their efforts have been rewarded.

15 September: Warm welcome

The next day, at the welcome press conference, Warren Gatland speaks warmly about the reception he and his players have received.

"I think it's fantastic, the way they've embraced Wales. Even down to having the dragon on fire engines around the city. I know they wanted to be a host city for the World Cup. We heard last night that there's been a significant uptake in the number of youngsters playing rugby, so we see that as being incredibly positive. And for the players to see all the flags and posters around town wishing Wales all the best – it's been quite humbling, really."

With the help of phonetically spelled song-sheets, the locals have been studiously learning the national anthem, together with Welsh hymn 'Calon Lân'. And in Wales captain Alun Wyn Jones, they already have a fan.

"We were lined up to sing 'Calon Lân' [at the airport] as well, but we changed our itinerary because they sang so well! But the welcome's been phenomenal, and in particular the schoolchildren singing was a highlight."

Gatland goes on to speak about the injured players. Adam Beard, we're told, is due to meet up with the squad on Thursday when they move on to Toyota, and could be in contention for the Australia game. Cory Hill, who's been training separately from the rest of the squad, should also be back in the selection mix for the Wallabies. Outside half Rhys Patchell, replaced during last weekend's defeat to Ireland, has been working through his concussion protocols, and should be fit for the start of the tournament.

The team have trained once already, and will be doing plenty this week. After the hot conditions in Switzerland and Turkey, they've already acclimatised to high temperatures. But Warren Gatland says they're taking no risks when it comes to the humidity expected at night-time.

"We've been using wet balls, and baby oil on some of the balls as well. The challenge is going to be to dealing with the slippery ball. Players who've been to New Zealand have experienced that, and a lot of these players have experienced night rugby as well, so I think they'll be able to cope with the conditions."

It's been an indifferent summer results-wise for Wales, with one victory and three defeats. But the Wales coach says they haven't yet shown their full hand, and will get better the longer they spend together. Previous campaigns suggest there's truth in this, and we know how Wales can gather some winning momentum.

It strikes me that the Australia game on 29 September could be a defining one. Win that, and they'll likely face an easier quarter-final. Lose, and a monumental tussle with England could be in the offing. Either way, it's not long before the serious stuff begins.

16 September: Red-letter day

We've been told there's an open training session today at Kitakyushu Stadium. It's expected to be well attended, especially since the locals have been denied an actual World Cup game. But nothing can prepare us for the scene when we get to the park just a stone's throw away from the ground.

It's filled with fans dressed in red WRU T-shirts, some supplementing the look with daffodil hats and fancy dress. Queues, hundreds of metres long, snake around the block and back again towards the stadium.

On a stage at one end of the park, two singers wielding microphones conduct the crowd in repeated singalongs of 'Hen Wlad Fy Nhadau' and 'Calon Lân'. Quite why they're doing this will soon become clear.

In amongst the melee, posing for pictures with fans, we find a contingent from the WRU, including ex-player Rhys Williams, now Business Development Manager with the union and one of those behind the engagement programme here in Kitakyushu.

"It's all been about building support for the team ahead of the Rugby World Cup," he says. "But in the meantime we're building the brand of rugby, especially Welsh rugby. Engaging with the citizens, coaching coaches, giving children of all ages and abilities the chance to have an experience of rugby. And hopefully when the team train later on, it'll be a huge surprise and boost to see the support."

We plough through the crowd to the stadium entrance. Training is due to start a 2.30 p.m., but has to be pushed back because of the volume of people. The ground, which normally hosts the local football team, has a capacity of 15,000, and looks set to be full to the rafters. It's more like match day in Cardiff than Monday in Kitakyushu. Supporters, brandishing their Welsh song-sheets, are eagerly belting out the anthem.

"I like the Welsh spirit," explains one man, brandishing his 'Go, go Wales' banner proudly. "I like 'Land of My Fathers'." He tells me about his trip to the Principality Stadium in Cardiff, before launching into a full-throated, and surprisingly accurate, solo rendition of '*Hen Wlad Fy Nhadau*'.

"There are many people here," agrees a young female fan. "But these days we have a TV drama about rugby, so maybe there are many younger and older women here!"

Eventually, the team, led by Alun Wyn Jones, run out onto the pitch. Cue a full-blooded and very musical rendition of the Welsh national anthem, followed by '*Calon Lân*'. Green-topped mountains loom in the background, serene in the afternoon sun. Maybe it's that rugged landscape, together with the city's history of industry and shipping, that helps its people identify so strongly with their guests.

Training is watched avidly, with every passage of play applauded. Gasps greet the up-and-unders hoisted by Dan Biggar and Rhys Patchell. As one player admits later, it's unusual to PLAY in front of crowd as big as this back home, never mind train.

Afterwards, clearly moved by the occasion, the squad do a lap of honour, tossing souvenir mini-balls into the crowd. I'm

29

pitchside with my camera, filming the crowds as they chant. It's a public holiday, and there are hundreds of children lapping up the moment. I can't quite believe the effort the people have put into today, and the joy they've had from the experience.

"It's just incredible," says Ryan Jones, former Wales captain and now WRU head of performance, another of those tasked with laying the ground for this visit.

"18 months ago, we set out with the ambition to turn the city red for when Wales arrived, and today's the culmination of all our effort, and the work that's been done with schools, universities, businesses, the public, chat-shows. The people have taken Wales and Welsh rugby to their hearts."

"To see the guys' faces as they came up from the changing room into this arena – they didn't know what to expect. They weren't expecting this and they've been blown away. Even talking to some of the staff, in all the years and all the World Cups they've been to, they've never seen anything like this."

Later that evening, there's an official World Cup welcome ceremony at the nearby convention centre.

For the players – applauded for the umpteenth time that day as they filter into the auditorium – it's probably all a bit overwhelming. Although they do look chuffed to receive their World Cup caps from WRU Chairman and World Rugby committeeman Gareth Davies. They're now officially part of rugby's biggest tournament.

Alun Wyn gives a gracious speech and takes part in a traditional painting ceremony, where he's asked to paint part of the head of a Japanese *Daruma* doll for good luck, after making a wish. What was the wish? Well, there can be only one answer.

"We've come here to give the best of ourselves and obviously do our utmost to win the World Cup."

Judging by today's turnout, they've earned themselves a whole load of new supporters.

17/18 September: Back to earth

Ah, Welsh rugby. From concord to chaos in just over 24 hours. Wasn't it ever thus? After the joyous but tiring day with the fans, Tuesday is supposed to be quieter. And, up until about 11 p.m., it is. We file our report for the day (a nice piece about a school visit featuring Ken Owens and Cory Hill), and then venture into town for some cold beers.

On our way for dinner, we spot some of our colleagues from BBC Wales and S4C in a bar, and decide to join them. Earlier, Luke Broadley, the Wales team Media Manager, alerted us to a story that would be breaking tonight: 'We are working to a 1 a.m. announcement Japanese time, but that could change,' he said, in a WhatsApp message distributed to the media.

My reaction is to expect injury news – perhaps that Adam Beard won't be joining the squad after all – and I think no more of it.

But when I casually mention this to our friends from the 'opposition', the atmosphere changes. We sense they're trying too hard to downplay the forthcoming announcement. 'I wouldn't be surprised if someone's just got a calf strain,' says one former player, now working as a pundit. They also seem suspiciously pleased with themselves. Moments later, I'm called out onto the street by Tom and Siân, who have been keeping across the news on their smartphones. By this point, we've enjoyed a few drinks and are, shall we say, a little merry. 'It's about Rob Howley,' says Tom. 'He's being sent home.' I look at him blankly. He hands me the phone and I read the headline: 'Wales assistant coach to be sent home after being accused of betting on matches.' It takes a few seconds for the words to register. I check my phone. There's no official word from the WRU yet, but it would appear a rather large story is about to break.

We make our excuses to the Beeb/S4C contingent. As they're having a few beers, I presume they've known about this for a while and have already filed their stories for the evening bulletins. Back in Cardiff, our news desk is cottoning on to what's happening. It's about 4 p.m. there, and they're asking for a live report into Wales at Six, at 2 a.m. local time.

We need to eat, and maybe drink something non-alcoholic. Over barbecued food and large cokes at the next-door restaurant, we formulate a plan of attack. Siân will go and fetch the Live U (the piece of kit we use to transmit live), I will get suited and booted, and the four of us (including our fixer, Tristan) will head to an overpass overlooking the team hotel, by now of course shrouded in darkness, to bring the people of Wales the latest.

By now the WRU have released their statement: 'The WRU can confirm that Rob Howley has returned to Wales to assist with an investigation in relation to a potential breach of World Rugby Regulation 6, specifically betting on rugby union. The decision was taken to act immediately in light of recent information passed to the WRU. No further details can be provided at this stage as this would prejudice the investigation.'

It goes on to say that Stephen Jones, the Scarlets' attack coach, will be arriving 'imminently' in Japan to take over from Howley as assistant coach. On Wednesday (which by now, for us, it already is), WRU Chief Executive Martyn Phillips and Warren Gatland will be taking questions from the media.

I e-mail Dominic Rumbles, media relations man at World Rugby, who replies to tell me they'll also be issuing a statement this morning.

It's a bombshell, alright. And despite the lateness of the hour, it's not hard to convey the unfolding drama when we go live at 2 a.m. Less than 36 hours ago, Howley was on the pitch at Kitakyushu Stadium, drilling the players in front of 15,000 fans. Now he's back in Wales and feeling, I'd imagine, not very good about life. And just five days before Wales' World Cup opener, it's not a welcome development for the rest of the party, either. "This is highly embarrassing and highly disruptive," I tell Jonathan Hill, back in the studio two continents away. "I'm not sure how much light Martyn Phillips will be able to shed on matters."

A few hours later, a bleary-eyed press contingent gather at the team hotel to find out. Phillips, the WRU boss, starts the press conference by giving us some more information about the timeline of events. Last Wednesday, he says, the union were approached by the 'integrity team' from one of the betting companies. Further information was supplied on

33

Friday. By Sunday, Phillips felt there was justification to fly out to Japan. On Monday, after the open training session, he and another executive from the WRU sat down with Howley. After a second meeting, all agreed that he should return home to face a formal process.

Phillips says that Wednesday's information only reached the union after the squad were already en route to Japan, and adds that Rob's welfare, as a WRU employee, is a key consideration. Phillips won't be drawn on the specifics of what Howley's accused of, but confirms that he won't be returning to the Wales camp during the World Cup. He says that the squad have received an 'integrity briefing' from World Rugby since the news, but that this is not related to what's happened, and is something all teams get at the start of a World Cup. He's confident that the Wales players and management understand their responsibilities.

Alongside him, a wan-looking Warren Gatland admits to feeling "shocked" by the turn of events. But he says the team must move swiftly on and concentrate on the first match, which is in less than a week's time. Stephen Jones, a familiar face from the Gatland era, won't take long to get up to speed, he adds. The Wales coach praises the senior players, who he says have "stepped up" and taken responsibility since Howley's departure.

Dan Biggar and Jonathan Davies, sent in next to face the media, say it's simply a case of keeping the ship afloat. "For Monday night, a lot of the framework has already been done and we'll probably stick to what we've planned for that," says the Wales outside half. 'But I'm sure the longer Steve is in camp and the more comfortable he gets, the more he'll bring his own ideas.'

I head back to the hotel to file my report. I've actually been impressed with the WRU's response to this. They've fronted up to the press and not tried to cover anything up. In doing so, they've drawn the sting from a potentially very damaging story. And, in the cold (or warm) light of day, I actually think this mini-crisis could be a galvanising force. As Biggar said earlier, it wouldn't be the first time the players have had to deal with off-field distractions (who could forget the Ospreys/ Scarlets 'merger' story that unfolded during the Six Nations this year). As then, perhaps this incident could make it even easier for them to focus on the task in hand. And personally, I think Stephen Jones' arrival will do no harm. He's an ebullient character, and his work as Scarlets' attack coach has won many admirers.

Heading out for dinner, we're left to reflect on a contrasting few days in Kitakyushu. From the excitement of open training on Monday to the extraordinary events of Tuesday and Wednesday, it feels like we've experienced Welsh rugby in microcosm: from glorious highs to devastating lows. That said, I'm not sure I'd want a repeat over the next six weeks. It's a bit like riding a rollercoaster: exhilarating, but you're always glad to get off.

4

Nagoya / Toyota

19 September: The age of the train

Feeling rather bedraggled after the exertions of the last few days, we check out of the hotel and head towards the train station. It's a short walk without luggage, but with four heavy bags each and in the hot morning sun, it's a slog. I'm starting to realise that this trip will be a physical as well as a mental challenge. We've been in Japan a week, and it already feels like a month.

Like beasts of burden, we make our way through the crowds at the busy Kokura Station to the ticket office, and from there onto the platform. We're bound for Nagoya, Japan's fourth largest city. But the morning's stress evaporates when, on the stroke of 12:31, the *shinkansen* (bullet train) glides up on the tracks, needle-nosed and gleaming in the sunshine, ready to bear us to back to Honshu, Japan's main island.

Powered by electricity and reaching speeds of up to 200 mph, the Japanese bullet trains were the first of their kind in the world. And this afternoon, reclining in our comfortable seats and mopping our brows with complimentary hot flannels, there seems no finer way to travel. Baggage safely stowed, I nap while we speed silently through the countryside.

In a few hours, we'll reach Shin-Osaka, where we're due to change for Nagoya.

It's hard not to compare negatively with rail travel back home. Even in economy, the carriages are wide, spacious and clean. No one comes to inspect our tickets. No one's babbling annoyingly on their mobile. According to Wikipedia, in the 50+ years the *shinkansen* have been operating – during which time over 5.3 billion passengers have used them – there's never been a single fatality due to a train accident.

And, not for the first time, we're struck by the unique Japanese sense of courtesy. Whenever a train employee leaves or enters our carriage, they turn to face us, and bow elaborately. It's a lovely, almost courtly gesture, evocative of a bygone age, even if it can seem slightly odd to western eyes.

After manhandling the bags from one train onto another and then off again, we arrive in Nagoya. The ageing taxi driver (most of the drivers seem to be on the mature side of 60) wrestles manfully with my massive suitcase, ramming it in onto the passenger seat alongside him. During the journey, I have to lean precariously though the gap between the front seats to stop it from toppling into his lap.

Finally, we're ensconced in the Crowne Plaza Hotel, our home for the next five nights. This being a travel day, there's no work to do, so we adjourn to the Sky Bar on the thirtieth floor for pre-dinner beers. Panoramic views stretch out on all sides as dusk settles over the urban sprawl. Somewhere out there, to the south-east, lies Toyota, where Wales will finally make their World Cup bow on Monday night.

21 September: Better with age

At last: the show is on the road, the balloon has gone up. After the interminable build-up, the training, the warm-up games, the Howley affair, Wales are about to get some rugby.

For others, it's already started. Last night we watched Japan overcome a nervous start to beat Russia in Tokyo, earning a bonus point in the process. Today, we've seen Australia and Fiji, Wales' Pool D rivals, go toe to toe, with the Wallabies seeing off a spirited showing from the islanders to win 39-21. France almost imploded before overcoming Argentina 23-21. And this evening, a devastating two-try burst from the All Blacks derailed the challenge of South Africa. Everywhere you look, gauntlets are being thrown down, stalls set out.

For Wales, the last of World Rugby's tier 1 teams to enter the fray, the waiting's nearly over too. Today, the team to take on Georgia in Toyota was named. As expected, it's strong. Unexpectedly, it doesn't contain Ross Moriarty in the back row – "some things to work on," says Warren Gatland – or Nicky Smith at loose-head prop. Instead, there are starts for Wyn Jones up front and the impressive young flanker Aaron Wainwright, with Josh Navidi packing down alongside him at number 8. And it's a big night for Alun Wyn Jones, due to win his 129th cap and go joint top, with Gethin Jenkins, in the all-time list for Wales appearances.

"To rub shoulders with Melon [Jenkins] on this one is pretty sweet, although I'm expecting a satirical message from him! The biggest thing I can do to mark the occasion is to go out and enjoy the game and have a good win. That's the focus."

At 34, and showing no sign of slowing up, there could be many more for the Osprey, who also has nine Lions caps. Even Warren Gatland, not a man easily given to gushing, is impressed.

"He's got better with age, like a wine," the Wales coach tells the media, with a distinctly uncomfortable-looking Alun Wyn alongside him. "The pleasing thing is that, over the last couple of years, he's been recognised worldwide and not just in Wales. People realise what a contribution he's made with his performances, leadership and captaincy."

Unusually, today Tom and I watch the whole of the Wales training session, as opposed to the usual ten minutes of 'open training' allotted to the media. It's notable how hard the players are working. Those not in the match-day squad of 23 are made to do shuttle sprints by fitness coach Paul Stridgeon. In these humid conditions, where even walking can be draining, it looks murderous. On another part of the field, Ken Owens, Navidi and scrum half Gareth Davies rehearse a set move off the line-out. We wonder if that might feature on Monday.

This evening, we spot our first Wales fans of the trip, near our hotel back in Nagoya (about an hour's train ride from Toyota). We expect many more to be arriving over the coming few days. It'll be interesting to hear what they make of it all.

Personally, I've enjoyed the food. In common with many Japanese workers, we've generally been eating at *izakayas* – a sort of pub/restaurant. Here, customers order a selection of small dishes – for example *sushi*, *wagyu* beef, *edamame* or *tempura*. Helpfully, there's a button at the table to summon the waiter. The food is washed down by lashings of Asahi or Sapporo beer.

To the Western eye, it's surprising how much alcohol the typical 'salaryman' (or woman – the Japanese name for a white-collar worker) drinks on a weekday evening. But in Japan, after-work drinks with colleagues are an important part of the culture. Many Japanese drinkers lack the necessary enzyme to break down alcohol, so tolerance can be low. But for those wishing to avoid a hangover, help is at hand. *Konbini*, or convenience stores, sell a selection of bottled hangover cures. Necking one before an evening out is thought to offset the after-effects the next morning.

It might have been wise to have one of them this evening, I reflect, as I get ready for a game of darts at a local sports bar. It's not the traditional variety of the game, with a wooden board and steel arrows, but a neon incarnation, with a board which lights up when you hit it.

Only in Japan.

23 September: A solid start

Game day dawns, and the weather is set fair for Toyota. Yesterday there was stormy weather in the forecast, and with the retractable roof on the Toyota City Stadium not in use since 2015 due to maintenance costs, the players were preparing themselves for wet-weather conditions. But today the sun is shining and looks here to stay.

By now, the matches are coming thick and fast. Last night England huffed and puffed before eventually winning with a bonus point against Tonga. Earlier, Ireland had crushed

Scotland in a clinical display in Yokohama. Italy also seemed in fine fettle, sweeping past Namibia with seven tries, though with New Zealand and South Africa in their pool, there are tougher times ahead for the *Azzurri*. There's plenty to chew over as we convene for our lunch of chicken *katsu* curry.

The train is much busier than it's been before, with Welsh fans filling the carriages. Arriving at Toyota, the street in front of the station is already a sea of supporters, with many locals getting into the festival atmosphere. There's a group of Japanese guys dressed as samurai swordsmen. Two Japanese girls dressed as geishas walk by. White headbands inscribed with Japanese writing are handed out for Welsh fans to wear. At the packed bar near the Wales team hotel, a red-shirted crowd are belting out 'Delilah' at the tops of their voices. It's almost like match day in Cardiff.

The fans we speak to have certainly enjoyed a warm welcome in this faraway land. "They're a fantastic nation – very, very polite," says one man from north Wales. "They've been lovely," adds another visitor. "Everywhere we've gone they've been really friendly. The language is a problem, for us as well as for them, but it doesn't matter."

It's time to walk to the stadium, a space age-looking construction reached by crossing an impressive bridge. At the nearby park, there's some kind of stunt demonstration taking place, with the sound of motorbikes revving, and a large ramp in place.

In the press room, I bump into Shane Williams, part of the ITV Sport team out here to cover the game. Last weekend, he was in Tenby, competing in the annual Ironman triathlon.

Last year, he finished the race in just over 11 hours, a pretty impressive effort for an amateur. All in a day's work for Wales' record try-scorer.

There's a bit of a faff as I attempt to locate our seats for the game. By the time I find someone who can help, half an hour has passed. Then I'm lost, and have to jog around the outside of the stadium to get back to the press room. By the time I get there, sweating in my smart shirt, I'm not in the best of moods. At least my magical mystery tour has allowed me to admire the scene outside, with fans flooding over the bridge beneath a fiery Japanese sunset.

Inside the ground, it's an equally impressive spectacle. It's the highest stadium I've ever seen, with stands soaring upwards into the night sky. The pitch looks pristine, and the conditions are mild and still, perfect for spectating. There are few empty seats in the 45,000-seater arena.

And there's plenty for them to cheer. After just two minutes, Jonathan Davies scythes through some porous Georgian defence to run in unopposed. Ten minutes later, off a set move, Josh Adams is through. From the ruck, Justin Tipuric shows dancing feet to dot down under the posts.

The next try is almost a carbon copy, with Adams himself this time supplying the finish. And when Liam Williams collects a bouncing ball to score the fourth, it's 29-0 going into half-time, and Wales have their bonus point.

The momentum slows a little in the second half, with the Georgians showing some fight; but two more tries, from George North and replacement Tomos Williams, put the gloss on a 43-14 scoreline.

It seems a case of job done: Wales wanted to show improvements in attack, and with six tries they've done just that. Even Rob Howley, back in Bridgend, might have allowed himself a smile at the ease with which the backs opened up the Georgian defence.

Afterwards, Warren Gatland says he's "pretty pleased" with the bonus point, and the chance to replace key players early ahead of the next game. Dan Biggar says the team were "really good" in launching first-phase attacks. But everyone knows there's a sterner test to come.

"We're probably a bit disappointed, if I'm honest, with the second half," says Alun Wyn Jones. "We let a couple of tries in. It's a good result but there's plenty to work on."

Following the game, I find myself pitchside with Shane and Jamie Roberts, old teammates for Wales and the Lions. They agree that Wales have made a positive start, though acknowledge that Georgia, in the first half in particular, were not at their best. Both say Tipuric was outstanding. Roberts points out his role in Wales's last try, where his harrying of the Georgian kicker led to the fluffed effort from which Tomos Williams was able to set up George North.

On air, I ask him about our prospects against Australia in six days' time.

"The game's going to be crucial in deciding who finishes first and second in the group, and who makes it through to the semi-final and final. It's very tough to call. I think it'll be a one-score game."

There are some injury concerns, it's revealed afterwards. Hadleigh Parkes has broken a bone in his hand, but it's hoped this won't keep him out of the Australia game; likewise Ken Owens, who's hurt his knee. Cory Hill is struggling to recover from his leg fracture and could be heading home tomorrow – an announcement will be made in the morning.

Afterwards, Tom, Siân and I go out to a now-deserted bridge to record our links for the news. By now, it's around midnight. On our way back to town, the party is still in full swing, although it's taken a toll on some of the fans. By the time we eventually get a cab back to Nagoya, it's after 2 a.m.

I'm left to reflect on a solid start for the men in red, though they'll have to do better on Sunday. As an event, tonight's been excellent, though the atmosphere was very different to the Principality Stadium on match day; at times it was so quiet we could hear the players shouting. And in the second half at least, the neutrals were all cheering for Georgia. It seems they love the underdog here.

Still, Wales have done what they needed to. It's early days, but they're top of Pool D. Later today they, and we, are off to Tokyo, where the Wallabies lie in wait.

5

Tokyo revisited

25 September: View from the inside

Some more facts about Tokyo: it has the busiest railway station in the world (Shinjuku Station, with over 3.6 million people passing through each day); the tallest tower in the world (Tokyo Skytree, at 634 m/2,080 ft); and more 3-star Michelin restaurants than anywhere else (good luck with eating at one of those on a journalist's budget!). Shinjuku Station gets so busy that staff have to physically push passengers on board at rush hour, and at Shibuya Crossing, an estimated 2,500 pedestrians cross the street at any one time. Yet this evening, in the heart of this mighty metropolis, I find myself in a small black tent surrounded by Welsh people.

It's the GlobalWelsh 'cwtch', a get-together for business folk and other Welsh movers and shakers who are in town to watch the World Cup. There's also a smattering of star names from the rugby world. Outside, I get chatting to Wayne Pivac, who'll be taking over the reins as Wales coach when Warren Gatland departs after this tournament. Pivac is optimistic about our chances against Australia on Sunday. He's also pleased about Stephen Jones being called up to replace Rob Howley as attack coach – it's a chance for Jones to get to know the set-up before he takes over for real as part of the new team. The Kiwi seems like a nice guy. I bet he's nervous, though: following in the footsteps of Wales' most successful coach of the professional era is quite a tall order.

After presentations from Welsh businesses hoping to make a mark in Japan, there's a Q & A featuring the famous faces. This is strictly 'off the record' so I'll not reveal who said what, but there's an interesting discussion on how to make the game safer, given the glut of injuries and the accent on dangerous tackles we've already seen at this World Cup (earlier today, Australian winger Reece Hodge was handed a three-week ban for his challenge on Fiji's Peceli Yato). One suggestion from the stage (perhaps made tongue in cheek) is to make pitches bigger, though it's acknowledged that this course of action would be costly. Another is to ban replacements. The argument goes that unleashing a pumped-up, 18-stone athlete on tiring players can only lead to trouble.

It's not the first time we've found ourselves privy to the unfiltered thoughts of a rugby notable since our arrival here. Last night, while out enjoying a belated celebration of the Georgia win, we found ourselves in an Irish bar, sitting near a Wales squad member and his family. He clearly didn't recognise us, and we ended up overhearing the conversation. It's fair to say his experience of the trip so far isn't entirely positive. There's apparently too little time off, too little to do, and the players are being kept on too short a leash. One player has got into trouble for not wearing the sponsor's training gear. There are restrictions on social media use. How true all this is, we'll never know (from what I've seen, the players seem to be pretty active on Twitter), but it's an interesting insight into real life behind the Wales PR machine. The time away from home, the media scrutiny, the pressures of selection... I imagine all these things can be challenging for the players, especially those not involved in the match-day squad. I suppose it's the management's responsibility to keep everyone feeling involved and important. But they've got plenty of tournament experience, and they seem to know what they're doing.

Since I've just mentioned Fiji, Wales' Pool D rivals were on the wrong end of the first big World Cup shock today, beaten by minnows Uruguay. With two defeats from two, the islanders are almost certainly out of the tournament after just six days. Does this mean they'll have downed tools by the time they face Wales in Oita, or will they be even more fired-up for a face-saving win?

I think I know the answer!

26 September: The kindness of strangers

With the big game just three days away, today there was good news on the injury front. Ken Owens and Hadleigh Parkes will both be fit for selection, although Parkes will be playing with a heavily strapped hand after breaking a bone against Georgia. As expected, Cory Hill has gone home after failing to recover from his leg injury. He's been replaced by Bradley Davies, who's flown out to join the squad.

At the squad's vast hotel in Tokyo (which seems to stretch over acres and contains its own shopping arcade), Robin McBryde tells us that although Wales will take confidence from last November's win over Australia, Sunday's game – in the rarefied atmosphere of the World Cup – will be a very different proposition.

"We'll take heart from the fact we know we can beat them. But these are different circumstances. This is the World Cup, with a lot more at stake. It's going to be a good battle."

Lock Jake Ball, official player of the match against Georgia and a dead cert to pack down again alongside Alun Wyn against the Wallabies, agrees. The Scarlets man has taken advantage of injuries elsewhere in the squad to cement his position in the first XV.

"I haven't missed many training sessions and I feel in a good place," says the big man. "I've been given the confidence to go out there and do what I do."

We're supposed to be hearing from Owens today as well, but precisely an hour after the start of the press conference, the hotel staff start stacking chairs and clearing up around us. The WRU have only paid for an hour's use of the room, and their time is up. For all their courtesy and good manners, we're also finding that the Japanese people are sticklers for rules and punctuality... at least it means their trains run on time.

After a lunch of *tempura*, I take a taxi to training. It's being held at the Prince Chichibu Memorial Rugby Ground – named after the brother of Emperor Hirohito, and the headquarters of the Japan Rugby Union. Inside, the players are very much in business mode after a couple of days off, and focused on their work. I see no sign of second-row duo Bradley Davies and Adam Beard, and assume they're resting. Far from it – they're being put through their paces by the fitness staff inside, according to Wales' media man. The aim, I'm told, is to ensure all the players reach the same training load, whether they're on the pitch or not.

I file my report for the day, then head out to meet up with Siân, who along with Tom has had a busy day filming for a piece known unofficially as '24 hours in Tokyo'. After visiting a fish market and the street-fashion district of Harajuku, this evening she's at a bar where they serve *shōchū*, a Japanese liquor distilled from rice. After the filming, we try some of the bluish liquor, said to be as strong as 40% ABV. It's my second taste of something like *sake*, and it's not growing on me.

After staying a while to chat to Koko, our rice wine expert, we ask for the bill for our snacks and drinks, only to find that a man at the bar has already settled it. He says it's important to Japanese people to show hospitality, and regales us with stories about the time he spent working in the UK. He's even heard of the DVLA in Swansea. It's another quite stunning display of kindness to us foreigners, far from home.

Down in Kobe this evening, England have not been in such a friendly mood, handing out a 45-7 defeat to the USA. The match saw American John Quill sent off for a dangerous tackle on English outside half Owen Farrell. The replay shows it's a fair call, but it's further evidence that this is a World Cup where tackle technique will be firmly in the spotlight.

27/28 September: Sky high

It's nearly 2 a.m., and I think I might be about to be part of a world first. I'm 400 metres or so up in the Skytree – the world's tallest tower – far above the city lights. From up here, even skyscrapers look like matchsticks. In a few moments, we're about to go live on *Wales At Six*.

I'm sure I'm not the first person to report live from here (it is a broadcasting tower, after all), but I can't imagine there have been many who have done it at this hour. Not long after midnight, we met the three friendly folk who are to be our guides for the evening, in the plaza 1,000 feet below. We craned our necks as they told us how the viewing platform far above had been lit up red in our honour. Then we were escorted into the deserted building and up the elevators, ears popping, to our position two thirds of the way up the giant structure. At 634 metres high, it's not much shorter than Pen y Fan.

It's a surreal end to what's been another busy day. At lunchtime, Warren Gatland named an unchanged starting XV to take on the Australians on Sunday. The only change is on the bench, where Owen Watkin replaces Leigh Halfpenny as cover for Hadleigh Parkes, should the latter's injured hand prove problematic. There are apparently disgruntled players in the wider squad, and it's shown up in training, where blood has been spilled.

"There's been a few guys frustrated with selection, which is a good thing," Alun Wyn tells the press. "That breeds competition in the squad. There was a bit of red stuff flowing yesterday, which was well meant, because it's for the betterment of the team."

It's a game that Wales have been building up to for more than two years, ever since the World Cup pools were announced in May 2017. The match will likely decide the group winners, and the team set to avoid England and New Zealand in the quarter-finals and semi-finals. But Gatland is, in public at least, playing down its significance.

"We haven't really looked too far ahead," he says. "If you do get out of the group, the quarter-finals and semi-finals are all going to be pretty tough games. It's really about taking one game at a time and trying to build and create momentum, and we feel that we're a team capable of doing that. The longer we go on in tournaments, we feel we get better and more cohesive."

There's more praise for his skipper, who, all being well, will become Wales' most-capped player on Sunday.

"Since he's been captain, we don't have as many fights at training because he used to start most of them! That's how competitive he is. He doesn't say a lot, just leads from the front at training and in matches and sets a great example for the players. We're very lucky to have him captaining the side."

There's also a question about the game's hot topic: the World Rugby guidelines on dangerous tackles. Australia coach Michael Cheika has been scathing about the ban handed to Reece Hodge, saying none of his players believed what he did "met the red card threshold", and it's an issue that seems to be dividing pundits and confusing referees. Gatland, no doubt mindful of the potential for one of his own players to find themselves on the wrong side of the man in the middle, advocates a common-sense approach.

"I feel for Reece in terms of what's happened. You saw the incident in real time and it didn't look like much. Then you go to replays and slow it down and it looks a bit more sinister.

In the heat of battle, players do get themselves caught in the wrong position or make a mistake. You need a bit of sympathy for some of those things, but we're continually driving home the message to the players about discipline."

Back at our hotel, the Shinjuku Hilton (or 'Hil-ton' to taxi drivers, baffled by our pronunciation), the lobby is increasingly filled by the red and gold hues of the supporters. Rhys and Fraser, two friends originally from Pencoed, now reunited for a good old-fashioned rugby tour, wax lyrical about the fun they're having in Tokyo. They recommend the Golden Gai district with its miniature bars, the "maddest" place they've been. Dave, from Sydney, looks resplendent in his green and gold blazer. Tom and I join him and his seven Aussie friends to do some filming on the hotel terrace, now a dedicated rugby bar.

"I think it's going to be an absolute arm wrestle," he tells us. "These two teams have been neck and neck for about five years or so. We've won 13 [of the last 14 games], you guys have won one, but the results have been close. Wales are the best defensive team in the world; Australia are one of the world's best attacking teams. I think it could go either way."

His mate Simon, equally knowledgeable about the game, reckons the Wallaby fans will struggle to outvoice the Welsh on Sunday, despite their best efforts.

"The singing is going to be unbelievable. I must admit that you guys are much better singers than us."

They then blast out a full-throated rendition of 'Advance Australia Fair' (including the second verse) as if to prove their musical credentials.

I edit my piece, we eat, then it's off across town for our midnight rendezvous at the Skytree. 1,200 feet up, feeling a little faint with tiredness, we make conversation with our Japanese guides as we get ready to go on air. One produces a detailed manual about the building's design, which we feel obliged to study intently by torchlight. It's the early hours, but they seem very awake. On air, I tell the story of the generosity of the man in the bar the night before. The kindness of the locals is, deservedly, becoming a theme of the trip.

Afterwards, as if we needed more evidence of that, our new friends shepherd us to our taxi, and hand us a goody bag to take away. I'm exhausted when I get back to the hotel, and fall asleep as soon as my head hits the pillow.

*****

Later that afternoon, Tom and I hunt out a bar where we can watch the Japan v. Ireland game. They say all tournaments need a shock, and the Brave Blossoms are becoming adept at them. After showing up the Springboks in Brighton back in 2015, today they're at it again, overcoming an early deficit to defeat the world's number 2 team 19-12.

It's an inspiring display from the host nation, who launch wave after wave of attacks at the visibly shaken Irish. In the pub, the local fans (and the neutrals, like us), cheer wildly. At the final whistle, the old Japanese man next to me puts down his pipe and orders champagne for everyone. It's a big blow to Ireland's hopes of winning Pool A and avoiding an encounter with the All Blacks in the quarter-final.

That night we take the advice of our Welsh friends and head to the Golden Gai to do some celebrating of our own. The bars are indeed tiny – the size of a modestly sized front room – and it takes us a while to find one that will seat us all. When we do, we find ourselves in the company of two garrulous Aussies. As the beer and *sake* flow, both sides downplay their own team's chances for the following day. Personally, I've given up trying to predict the outcome. There's rain in the forecast, which may help Wales; and Australia have made changes, picking a conservative-looking side, which may suggest they're concerned about us. But history shows these are tightest of affairs, and who's to say it won't be the same tomorrow.

29 September: Ways to win

I'm no nearer picking a winner the next morning at breakfast, or when sitting in the sauna of the hotel's traditional Japanese bathhouse, sweating out the booze from the night before. The train ride from Shinjuku to Tokyo Stadium offers no fresh insights; nor does the sweltering walk from the station to the ground. Inside, ensconced in the 'TV room', I search the faces of the former players now working for Australian sports networks – legends like George Gregan and Tim Horan. If they're any the wiser, they're not letting on. Sometimes, you just have to let events pan out. As I take my seat in the media tribune overlooking the pitch, I feel strangely calm.

Despite our Aussie friend's claims about the singing the other night, it's the Wallaby fans who seem to be making the most noise during the anthems. But the Welsh have more to cheer when the game gets underway. From the kick-off, the Wales forwards rob Australia of the ball, and Dan Biggar drops back into the pocket and snaps a drop goal. 3-0. For the next ten minutes, the sides size each other up like prizefighters: a raid here, a thrust there. Then Wales launch a series of attacks off a line-out. Alun Wyn is tackled high, and the French referee signals a penalty. From the advantage, Biggar lofts a cross kick, weighted beautifully, as if with a nine iron onto the green... Hadleigh Parkes, right hand strapped heavily, outjumps his opponent, shifts the ball to his left paw, and scores. Biggar's conversion bisects the post. 10-0.

Too good to be true? Yes. The men in gold haven't come here to roll over. Bulldozing centre Samu Kerevi is imposing himself. He's brought down near the line but the Welsh defence is scrambling to reorganise. Bernard Foley spots space and launches a diagonal of his own. Out on the wing, Adam Ashley-Cooper catches, stumbles, but gathers himself to score. Foley misses the conversion but soon slots a penalty. 10-8. And there's worse news for Wales: Biggar is off for a Head Injury Assessment after throwing himself at Kerevi. He doesn't look like coming back.

This is a big test for Rhys Patchell. He's had an up-and-down time with Wales, the Scarlets outside half: excellent against Argentina last summer, exposed by Eddie Jones and England in the 2018 Six Nations. Now here he is, pulling the strings for his team in one of their biggest matches. He's soon on the scoreboard after Australia are penalised for hands in the ruck. Moments later, he's flattened by Kerevi in midfield. There's a lengthy delay as the officials review the replay.

Eventually, the big Australian gets a talking-to for leading with his forearm, and Patchell steps up for another shot at goal, this one from long range. Over it goes. 16-8.

Then, with just five minutes till the break, Wales strike a hammer blow. From the line-out, Will Genia's pass is a fraction slow and Gareth Davies intercepts, the Wales scrum half outsprinting the cover defence to score under the sticks. The Aussie alongside me says he's offside, which seems a fair shout, but replays show it's simply great anticipation and speed from the Wales no. 9. Patchell's conversion means it's 23-8 at half-time. On my way to the press room, I see Jamie Roberts: "The game's done," he says.

If only. Shortly after Patchell stretches the Welsh lead with another drop goal, Matt To'omua comes on for Foley. There's an immediate increase in tempo from Australia. After prolonged pressure, Dane Haylett-Petty goes over for a try, converted by To'omua. Then, from a scrum, Wales launch a botched blindside move. They don't see the ball for what seems an age. The Wallabies go through phase after phase, battering the Welsh line. It's inevitable they'll score. They do, via captain Michael Hooper. To'omua adds the extras, and when he strokes over a penalty five minutes later, it's a one-point game.

The ghosts of a decade of defeats start to circle. Spectres from Sydney. Phantoms from the Principality Stadium. 'Waltzing Matilda' echoes around the Tokyo evening. In an apocalyptic twist, even a section of the floodlights conks out. Is the meter about to run out on another Wales performance? Will they valiantly fall short again when it really counts?

Not this time. From a rare foray into Australian territory, they win a penalty. Patchell, man of the moment, steps up to stroke it home. 29-25. Moments later, Australia win a penalty. They kick for the corner. Tomos Williams, on for Gareth Davies, leaps like a salmon to keep the ball in play, denying the Wallabies a line-out deep in Welsh territory. There's still time for a last assault. This is where the hard work counts. The floggings in Fiesch in the Swiss Alps, the horrors of the heat camp in Turkey. Liam Williams, quiet by his standards today, picks his moment to enter a ruck, and steals the ball. Wales now need to set up a couple of rucks and the clock will go red. Alun Wyn – who else? – does the honours. 80 minutes is up, and Tomos Williams hoofs the ball out. 29-25 Wales.

"In years gone, by I think we probably would have lost that game," says Ken Owens afterwards. "That's how we've grown and developed as a squad over the last two years. We've found ways to win." Jonathan Davies echoes the sentiment, hailing the "resilience" of the players. Gatland is all smiles: "We didn't have a lot of ball in the second half and Australia kept coming at us and putting us under an enormous amount of pressure. We were able to hold on, thankfully!"

The squad will no doubt play it down in the days to come, but make no mistake about the significance of this win. It's only the second time ever that Wales have beaten a Southern Hemisphere side in a World Cup (the other occasion being 32 years previously, when Wales beat the Wallabies in the third-place play-off). If they go through the pool unbeaten, it will be only the second time ever, since 1987, that they've done that. As I walk along the edge of the pitch to my interview position, it's easy to see how much it means to the players. Shane Williams, there for ITV Sport, is swept up in a sweaty bear hug by Alun Wyn.

"Wales were magnificent," says Jamie Roberts. "It's been two years in the making. Ever since the draw was made, this was the game that was likely to decide the winners of this pool. And Wales have one foot in the quarters."

It's been a wonderful few hours. As we travel back to Shinjuku on the train, we discuss how the evening's events might impact upon us. For a start, it looks like we might need to find some accommodation in Oita for the quarter-final.

Out in town that evening, the fans are loving life. Warren Gatland has said he wants the players to enjoy their evening, too. I'm sure they will, but I still get the sense that they're not getting too carried away. They want to keep improving, and keep winning. And the exciting thing is, I genuinely believe they will.

6

Otsu

1 October: Gatland's way

24 hours later, we're safely ensconced in the Wales hotel in Otsu. It's a world away from the tumult of Tokyo and the night before. In the last of the evening light, I look out from my balcony onto a peaceful scene: the waters of Lake Biwa lap gently against the shore, against a backdrop of green-topped mountains. As twilight falls, city lights flicker into life. For rest and recuperation, this will do nicely.

This has always been part of the plan: Wales, with nine days till their next match – against Fiji – wanted somewhere for the players to unwind after the busy first fortnight. Otsu, a sleepy resort half an hour from Kyoto, seems to fit the bill. The place is dominated by the lake, the largest in Japan. Pleasure boats cruise back and forth on the glassy surface. Fishermen cast their rods at the water's edge. An old man slowly cycles by.

The hotel, set on a small rise and with blue-tinted brickwork, resembles a large leisure centre. The blue-blazered staff, who look like they're straight out of a British seaside holiday camp, tend to an elderly clientele, here to soak up the last of the summer sunshine and enjoy the hotel's hot *onsen* (traditional

Japanese baths). The cleaners, dressed like a cross between WWI nurses and nuns, add to the sanatorium feel.

Today, Tuesday, is a day off for the players. But there is a press conference. Kicking coach Neil Jenkins says Dan Biggar is "fine" after his head knock. We also hear from Bradley Davies, fresh in Japan to replace the unfortunate Cory Hill. Bradley, known to be one of the squad's more humorous characters, looks a little dazed by the turn of events.

"I'd just finished in the gym and I had a missed call from Gats. I guessed then [about the call-up], unless I'd done something really bad! I called him back and he said, 'Can you jump on a plane tomorrow?' I went home, kissed my wife and kids goodbye and was straight in the car."

He says that he didn't deserve to be in the original 31-man squad, but is now feeling in great shape, and ready to play his part.

"My mindset was to go back [to the Ospreys, his region], keep fit and see how it goes. Obviously I'm not here to make the numbers up: I want to play."

We send our footage back to Cardiff, and drift out for a late lunch. Afterwards we wander round the amusement centre next to the hotel. Rhys Patchell and Wyn Jones are in the arcade, playing a video game. Upstairs, some of the fitness staff are tenpin bowling. Others have gone out to see the sights in the surrounding areas. There's a holiday mood.

Presumably the party would have had this break regardless of results. But it must feel especially sweet given how Pool D has panned out so far. Wales are top, with 9 points from 2 games, and well placed to progress to the quarter-finals as pool winners. That would mean they'd avoid New Zealand – and probably England – until the final. It's about as good as a position as they'd have dared hope for at this stage.

And how satisfying for the coaching team. This is what they've been building towards for four years. And with all of them – Stephen Jones excepted – moving aside after the tournament, they've got a chance to sign off in style.

None more so than the man at the top. In under 12 years, Warren Gatland has guided Wales to three Grand Slams, a Championship (with an honourable mention to Rob Howley here, who took charge while Gatland was away with the Lions), a World Cup semi-final, and a record-breaking 14-match winning streak. He's overseen five of only six Wales wins ever over South Africa, and now the first back-to-back victories against Australia since the 1970s.

How's he done it? According to centre Jonathan Davies, part of the set-up since 2009, it all starts with hard work.

"The World Cup camps are renowned for being tough, and they are tough. But afterwards you're always left physically feeling like you can do more on the rugby field. If you feel much fitter, you feel like you can keep working and keep performing at a high standard."

"Having been here for quite a while, it's always the same structure: we get into camp, we work extremely hard to make the game feel easier for us. You're tired and you're struggling when you're training, but you're grateful when the game comes because it doesn't seem that hard then."

"Your natural ability is natural, but your capacity to go out there and keep pushing yourself has to be tested and developed over time. You back your work ethic against anything else, really."

And that hard graft breeds belief.

"[Gatland] has developed a winning mentality. Before that, Welsh rugby didn't have the confidence to say 'we expect to win', but now we go into games with confidence because we've done the work and we know what's needed from us."

"Before the Ireland game this year, Gats was like, 'We're ready. I don't need to say anything else.' That was all that was needed. Because he knew that after the preparation over the previous eight weeks, we were in a spot where we knew exactly what we needed to do to win the Grand Slam."

And it seems the Wales coach isn't given to fits of temper in the changing room.

"At half-time in France [in the 2019 Six Nations, where Wales had trailed 16-0 at the break, but came back in the second half to win], there was no shouting or raving. We knew we hadn't played any rugby, we hadn't had any ball. And he knew that if we went out there and kept the ball for a little bit of time, we'd create opportunities against France. It's knowing the game, and knowing what's needed of us at half-time or before the game."

Over the almost 12 years of the Gatland era, the personnel have changed and the tactics have evolved. But talking to those inside the camp, it seems like the basic building blocks of his winning formula have stayed constant: a deep belief that the team can beat anyone, engendered by a massive work ethic. Here in Japan, it's a philosophy that's being stress-tested on the biggest stage. So far, it's holding firm.

That evening, I decide to go for a run. Ominous black clouds are gathering over the lake as I leave the hotel, and it begins to rain. Soon, it's absolutely pouring, warm water streaming from the heavens as I splash my way up Otsu's main street.

On my way back, drenched, I notice a pleasure boat leaving for an evening spin around the lake. Inside, lit up against the darkness, I spot a large group wearing red shirts. It's the Wales squad, out for an engagement. As I watch, the rain falls and lightning illuminates the sky. But despite the unfolding storm, everyone on board looks content as the boat glides effortlessly out onto the water.

2 October: Kyoto

Today, training is optional for the squad, but everyone takes the chance to get out on the field and keep the legs moving. There's another day off tomorrow, and then the hard work will start in earnest ahead of the Fiji game, down in Oita.

Fijian hopes of progressing in the tournament may be forlorn after their two defeats thus far, but Robin McBryde has seen enough from the islanders, both here and in the past, to take nothing for granted.

"They weren't at their best against Uruguay but in that first half against Australia, they showed glimpses of what they can do. On past experience, we know that if we give them any opportunities, they're good enough to take them. It'll be their last game and they'll want to go out with a bang."

We know we'll be busy soon enough, too, so today we take the chance to visit Kyoto, just down the road. From 794 to 1868, Kyoto was the capital of Japan and it's probably still the best showcase for ancient Japanese culture. It's a stunning city, known for its many beautiful Buddhist temples, traditional red-painted Shinto shrines, Zen rock gardens and imposing imperial palaces. The temple of Kiyomizu-dera, with its wooden stage overlooking a gorge brimming with multicoloured foliage, is particularly striking, and the narrow lanes, traditional wooden buildings and old-fashioned merchant shops of the preserved historic district of Higashiyama which surrounds it convey a real sense of what the old capital city would have been like.

The Gion district is still the centre of Japan's geisha culture – a culture that revolves around traditional arts such as fan-dancing and playing the *shamisen* (a traditional Japanese stringed instrument), and the incredibly intricate and formal tea ceremony, rather than something seedier, as many westerners mistakenly think. Nature never feels far away, either. In the afternoon, we visit the sanctuary at Arashiyama, home to a colony of Japanese snow monkeys. Later we take a walk through a bamboo grove, surrounded on all sides by fragile-looking trees that remind us, in case we'd forgotten, that we're in Asia.

Before we leave, we watch the closing moments of France's game against the USA, with the French leaving it late to pull away in a game they eventually win 33-9. Back in Otsu, we adjourn to a German-themed bar (frequented, as it turns out, by a large press contingent) for New Zealand v. Canada. As expected, the All Blacks make light work of the Canadians, scoring eight tries in a 63-0 win. But they're also guilty of a

Tom Brown-Lowe, Siân Thomas and our good friends, the bags.

Kabuki-cho, Tokyo by night.

Moyan Brenn

The ITV Wales team enjoying the 'robot restaurant' in Tokyo.

Siân Thomas

The 2019 Wales Rugby World Cup squad showing off their caps.

Kitakyushu – a home from home for the Wales squad.

15,000 fans turn out to watch training in Kitakyushu.

centre photo: Siân Thomas

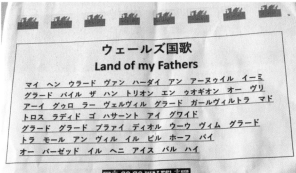

Japanese songsheet.

Kokura Castle, Kitakyushu.

Masgatotkaca

Tom, Siân and the author, enjoying some downtime in Kitakyushu.

Tristan Scholze

Japanese fans in Toyota ahead of Wales v. Georgia.

Pitchside at
Toyota Stadium.

Shibuya
Crossing, Tokyo.
Ben & Gab

Wales fans
before the
Australia game
in Tokyo.

Celebrating in the Golden Gai.

The Golden Gai, Tokyo by night.

Gzzz

Tokyo Skytree, a little earlier than our 2 a.m. live broadcast!

Kakidai

The ITV Wales team after our broadcast from Skytree.

Lake Biwa, Otsu.

Kiyomizu-dera Temple, Kyoto.

Martin Falbisoner

Geishas in the street in the Gion district of Kyoto.

top: Greg; bottom: David Offf

Lost in translation: this owl advert was one of many strange signs encountered in Japan.

The author interviews Hadleigh Parkes at Lake Biwa.

'The Welsh must be here.' A tempting invitation to drinkers in Oita.

Crowds at the unofficial fanzone in Oita for Japan v Samoa.

Jigoku or 'hell' in Beppu. Look out for Tom amidst the steam!

Food, glorious food: the team tuck into some tasty morsels in Oita.

The Brothers Davies face the cameras ahead of Wales v. Fiji.

Outside Oita Stadium before Wales v. Fiji.

The author with Fiji's Semi 'Semi Trailer' Radradra.

The author interviewing Rhys Patchell ahead of Wales v. Uruguay.

Siân Thomas

Beautiful Kumamoto at sunset.

The ghostly outline of how Oita castle might once have looked.

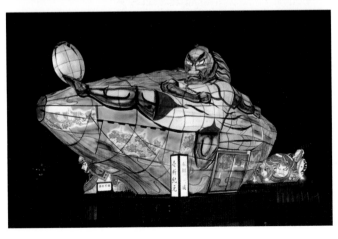

A *nebuta* float in Oita.

The author, Siân and Tom on the pitch at Oita after Wales v. France.

Warren Gatland and Alun Wyn Jones face the press ahead of the South Africa game.

Japanese fans show their appreciation for Dan Biggar and Alun Wyn Jones.

End of an era: Gatland shows his appreciation to the crowd and squad.

number of handling errors in the humidity of Oita – perhaps a warning to Wales, who play Fiji there, and a slight glimmer of hope to the other teams in the tournament.

4 October: Humble Hadleigh

It may be Friday, but with five days now till Fiji, Wales have entered 'match week'. And that means it's back to full tilt on the training ground. At lunchtime, as the players return from their morning 'run-out', we set up our cameras near the lake for an interview with Hadleigh Parkes. It's been quite a couple of years for the Kiwi: since making his debut for Wales back in 2017, he's become a mainstay of the side, and scored the opening try on Sunday, despite a broken bone in his hand.

"The mood's been really good [since the win over Australia]," he says. "But we're not getting ahead of ourselves either. It's about building from game to game, week to week. It's fantastic to be two from two, but as a group we want to be four from four."

I ask him if the players are buying into the excitement outside the camp, with supporters scenting a quarter-final against France, and a route to the last four.

He shakes his head. "If you start thinking about the bigger picture, that's when you might get turned over. That's why these next two games are important to us. [If we top our pool,] it does put us in a good position, but knockout rugby's a week-by-week game. Hopefully, come three or four weeks' time, we're still here and playing for the big one."

A New Zealander by birth, Parkes qualified for Wales by residency on 2 December, 2017. The same day, he scored two tries on his debut against South Africa. With another try in this year's Grand Slam game against Ireland, it's safe to say he's made an impact on the field. Off it, he says that the players are not just teammates, but friends too.

"There's not a person in the squad that I wouldn't want to have a coffee or even a beer with. Everyone's getting on really well; there's good belief and a good camaraderie. It's about wanting to do it for each other."

"I've had to pinch myself a few times. Playing for Wales is something I never believed would happen. I'm extremely privileged and humbled by the opportunities I've been given. It's been an amazing couple of years, and I'm loving every moment of it."

That evening, we're back in the German bar (our 'local') to watch South Africa dismantle Italy. Yesterday, Fiji reminded the rugby world of what they're capable of, putting Georgia to the sword in a 45-10, 7-try win. Wales have been warned.

After the Springboks game, it's off for dinner at the *izakaya* (restaurant/bar) across the road. Then we have a few games of tenpin bowling at the amusement centre next to the hotel. It gets quite competitive between the four of us (Siân's boyfriend, Aled, has by now joined the touring party), but we're all put to shame by the Japanese youngsters. They're clearly devotees of the game and rack up massive scores, often spinning the ball down, rugby-style, for extra effect. We're finding that when the Japanese people decide to do something, even as a hobby, they like to do it well.

In the morning we're moving on, and it's probably a good thing. Unlike the other places we've been, Otsu has felt outside the World Cup somehow – a sort of rugby limbo, where it's been hard even to find the games on TV. I feel relaxed, but ready to re-enter the fray. I suspect the team will be, too.

Tomorrow we head south to Oita, an area known for its bubbling springs and steamy atmosphere. Can Wales handle the heat against the Flying Fijians?

We'll soon find out.

7
Oita

5 October: Blooming Blossoms

Today sees our longest journey yet on the *shinkansen*: more than five hours with two changes – no mean feat given our mighty array of luggage. After changing at Shin-Osaka, we wend our way down to Kyushu and Kokura Station, scene of our first brush with the bullet train last month. It seems like an age ago. There, we pick up the JR Express train to Oita, a more rickety ride than we've been used to. By the time we arrive at our destination, I feel slightly bilious.

At least this time the hotel is right next to the station, so we don't face the usual task of loading the kit into two undersized taxis. And it looks nice, overlooking a large square, with trees lit up like Christmas. With lots of World Cup signage and artwork around, we feel we're back in the tournament mainstream after the quiet of Otsu. A billboard in the hotel advertises a nearby bar: "Why not drinking beer till 5:00 AM?", it asks. They must know the Welsh are in town.

There's a large unofficial fanzone nearby (in addition to the official one on the other side of the station), which is handy because Japan are in action this evening against Samoa. The change in atmosphere is palpable when the host nation takes to the field, with fans crowding the streets, sporting red and white jerseys. It's a mild Saturday evening, and there's a party mood, with supporters from Wales and Australia (the Wallabies played Uruguay here today) mingling with the locals, and cheering on every Japanese attack.

When the Brave Blossoms score their third try to make the game safe, the place erupts. When they score their fourth, to secure a bonus point and extend their lead at the top of Pool A, it explodes like the volcano Mount Aso, a few miles south of here. Fans are borne aloft, strangers embrace, and western and Japanese supporters exchange high fives. There's really nothing like seeing the host nation do well, particularly when they're underdogs, and now Japan are wonderfully placed to do what eluded them four years ago and progress to the last eight of a World Cup for the first time.

After the game we adjourn to a nearby *ramen* restaurant, where the celebratory mood continues. We munch contentedly on the thick noodles and try not to slurp the broth – although apparently doing so is encouraged as sign of enjoyment here in Japan. Table manners may vary by nation, but we're all enjoying this feast of rugby; and with just over a week of pool matches left in the race to reach the quarter-finals, there are many tantalising plot lines about to come to the boil.

6 October: Welcome to Hell

Talking of boiling, today we ventured to Beppu, just a short train journey down the coast, where Wales are based ahead of their game. Japan is located on the Pacific 'Ring of Fire', where many of the world's earthquakes and volcanic eruptions occur. Here, in this city shrouded by hot steam, where almost 3,000 hot springs spew out tonnes of scalding water, you feel nature's power close up. There's no media conference today, so we take the chance to explore.

Beppu has eight *jigoku* (literally, 'hells'), hot springs where water simmers in pools much too hot for a dip. A sulphurous smell hangs in the air. At the *Oniyama Jigoku* ('Devil Mountain Hell'), the steamy atmosphere is ideal for crocodiles, bred here for visitors to look at. Some sit, open-jawed, at the edge of the water. Others lurk, still and sinister, just beneath the surface. They're not my favourite creatures, but I feel sorry for them in their small ponds. The *Umi Jigoku* ('Sea Hell') is crocodile-free and we're allowed to bathe our feet. It's like a very hot bath, with water warm enough to redden the skin.

It's possible to enjoy an *onsen* (literally 'hot spring', but a term also used to describe the bathing facilities around it) in Beppu, but we don't have time. Luckily, I'm able to indulge at the hotel, which has a spa on the top floor. It's not my first time in the *onsen*, and I'm starting to get used to the experience. It's a bit like how I imagine a public bath would have been in Roman Britain. You go in, strip off (no bathing suits allowed), sit down on a stool and wash yourself (there's plenty of soap and shampoo on hand). Then, clean and rinsed, you enter the hot, mineral-infused water of the bath. It's incredibly relaxing.

Known as *hadaka-no tsukiai* ('naked friendship'), the *onsen* is seen as a great social leveller, a place where people from all walks of life can come together and chat, unencumbered by social station (or clothes). At most *onsen*, there are separate bathhouses for men and women, so striking up conversation is slightly less awkward.

For me, chatting's been non-existent, mostly owing to the fact that I don't speak Japanese. But I've found casting off my inhibitions quite easy – except for the time I visited the *onsen* in Otsu, at the hotel we shared with the Wales team. On that occasion, I waited till I knew the squad were out before venturing upstairs. If the players had spotted me, clad in my standard hotel-issue pyjamas and slippers, I'm not sure I'd ever have lived it down. Not that they're not keen themselves: I saw Shaun Edwards heading towards the spa one day, and a journalist colleague of mine, staying at a hotel in another part of the country, was enjoying his soak when half the Scottish squad came barrelling in.

So clearly, even rugby hard men enjoy a good *onsen*. Personally, I'm a convert. I think I'll find it hard to stop when I get home.

7 October: Brothers in Arms

For the Wales team, the time for relaxing is over. In just two days, they face the Flying Fijians. And today, at their hotel back in Beppu, we discovered which players had been picked for the job. As expected, it's another strong side. But there are changes: in the back row, Ross Moriarty gets a start at number 8, with Josh Navidi moving to the blindside flank. And James Davies, so full of fun when I met him at the Vale more than a month ago, replaces Justin Tipuric on the openside.

With James' brother Jonathan also in the starting XV, Wales will field a pair of brothers at a World Cup for the first time since 1999. Facing the cameras together, it's Jonathan, predictably, who plays the straight man to James' joker:

"I'm sure Mam and Dad are very proud – and the rest of the family," says Davies the elder. "But our focus is making sure we prepare well and get ready for a tough Test match against Fiji."

There's a brief pause while brother James is asked what he thinks.

"Yeah... what he said," comes the reply.

James is a little more expansive on the reasons behind his call-up for this match:

"I've just worked hard, really. You get disappointed at selection, but then it's about doing your best for the team. By working hard, it makes the team train better. And that's what I've done, I guess."

We're told that when James learned of his selection, he told Gatland that the Wales coach had "finally seen the light". It's a piece of cheeky self-confidence that Gatland admires:

"I thought that was brilliant. I have no problem with comments like that. It just says to me that players believe in their own ability and think they're good enough to be in the starting side."

And the Wales coach is under no illusions about the task ahead of them:

"We've had a good break, but it's going to be a tight game. [Fiji] are dangerous. We've just got to shut their space down and defend really well. Shaun's been speaking to the players all week about putting in an 80-minute performance defensively."

They'll need to. Fiji have named almost the same side which dismantled Georgia last week. And in wingers Semi Radradra and Josua Tuisova (nicknamed 'the Bus'), they boast two of the tournament's most terrifying attackers.

Not that we in Wales need reminding of the threat posed by the islanders. In 2007, I watched from the press box at Stade de la Beaujoire in Nantes, France, as Fiji flattened Welsh hopes of reaching the quarter-finals. That 34-38 defeat cost coach Gareth Jenkins his job, and remains one of the World Cup's great shocks.

Today, I catch up with another man with dark memories from that sunny afternoon.

"It was one of the toughest days in my rugby career," says Shane Williams, scorer that day of a sensational solo try. "Personally, I enjoyed the match. I played alright, scored a nice try and it went OK. But obviously we lost to a Fijian side that we thought we could match, playing at their own game. It didn't work."

It was indeed a wonderful spectacle, with nine outstanding tries. And while Shane senses Wales won't again be drawn into the kind of open game Fiji love, he still sees much to admire in the men from the South Seas, despite their shock defeat to Uruguay.

"I thought they were fantastic in the first half against Australia, and I really started to worry, knowing that Wales were going to play them. Individually, some of the best players in the world are in that team."

Still, Wales' record try-scorer is pleased with the way Wales are going about their business, too. Earlier, he had the chance to catch up with Gatland and Alun Wyn, away from the cameras.

"They're taking each day as it comes, but I like the air of the camp at the moment. It's very confident, and hopefully the momentum and the confidence will grow with each game."

At training back in Beppu, the players certainly look happy, enjoying a laugh as they gather for their pre-session huddle in the centre of the pitch. But watching them warm up, the lush mountains of Kyushu stretching behind into the distance, it's hard not to think they're in for another tough test of their credentials on Wednesday. Last week, Bradley Davies said the Fiji match at the 2015 World Cup was the hardest game of his life. Fiji may be out of this tournament, but they know a third-place finish in the pool will see them qualify automatically for the next World Cup in France, and history tells us they make Wales work hard for their wins.

As I stand in the sunshine watching training, a large butterfly – almost the size of a bat – ascends on the warm breeze, trying to surmount the netting that's been erected around the ground to deter prying eyes. Up and up it circles, but try though it might, it can't escape.

8 October: We Will Rock You

Today there's a bit of time off, so we visit the official fanzone. The unofficial one was great when Japan played Samoa on Saturday, and Tom and Siân found themselves caught up in an impromptu Japanese festival there the other night. But now, on the eve of the big match, it's time to see what the organisers have laid on here.

We wander around and enjoy the atmosphere, already building nicely 24 hours ahead of kick-off. There's a 'skills' area, where children take it in turns to run a rugby-related obstacle course, while volunteers toss balls around. Stalls sell local delicacies, as well as the more well-known brands associated with the tournament. In the marquee, red-shirted supporters are already availing themselves of liquid refreshment. There's a big screen to show the games, and a stage providing entertainment between times.

That afternoon, we settle down to watch Queeness, a tribute band to the rock group Queen. A small Japanese man does his best impersonation of Freddie Mercury, but may have been advised not to follow the famous singer in removing his shirt for the finale. He's not as svelte as Freddie, and it's hard not to concentrate on his quivering midriff as he belts out 'We Will Rock You' and 'We Are the Champions'. They're a good band, though.

Later, we return to the fanzone to watch South Africa see off Canada, before heading off to our favourite *ramen* joint in the company of Sarah Louisa, our GlobalWelsh friend from Tokyo. We're finding that we're often crossing paths with the same people on our odyssey around the country. The noodles go down well once again and we talk long into the night about our experiences so far, and the excitement ahead tomorrow.

9 October: "One of the most physical matches I've played"

It's another beautiful day, with blue skies and sunshine. A bit like Nantes, I reflect, as I wander across the square for a pre-match haircut. At the fanzone, the supporters seem to have forgotten all about that distant nightmare:

"I think we'll win by 30 points. It's not Fiji we have to worry about, it's the quarter-final, semi-final and final," says one bullish fan, his face invisible behind a samurai mask.

"It won't be 30 points – they don't want to push it," says another man, sporting a stuffed dragon named Dewi. "I think it'll be 25 points, something like that."

On the press bus to the stadium, there's a more restrained air, but no one, myself included, seriously expects Wales to lose. Yes, it was hard work back in Cardiff in 2015. But four years before that, we beat them 66-0. And anyway, that's all in the past. This streetwise Wales team won't be drawn into throwing the ball about as Fiji would like when keeping things tight will do the trick.

The futuristic dome of Oita Stadium heaves into view, and we make the long walk into the bowels of the stadium and the media room. Inside the ground – roof on – it feels cool and pleasant, ideal for running rugby. Today I'm on post-match interview duty with ITV Sport, so I'm sitting right next to the players' tunnel. I watch the two teams walk out onto the pitch. The Fijian boys look huge.

The game starts and Fiji have the first break, cutting through the Welsh line with alarming ease. There's a scrum on the right, and the ball goes blind to Tuisova. Josh Adams, his opposite number, tries and fails to tackle him. So does Dan Biggar. Josh Navidi, a massive man by anyone's standards, hits him with everything he's got, bundling Tuisova into touch. But not before he's grounded the ball in the corner. Ben Volavola misses the conversion, but it's 0-5 to Fiji.

Moments later they're over again, another sweeping movement putting in scrum half Frank Lomani. Fortunately for Wales, there's a forward pass in the build-up. But Ken Owens is off – sin-binned for a dangerous tackle – and shortly afterwards Fiji score again, this time Kini Murimurivalu proving too strong for Adams and his teammates. 0-10. But for a forward pass and some wayward kicking, it could have been much worse. There are 9 minutes on the clock.

Nantes, Nantes, Nantes. It's all I can think about. Wales must score next. They do: Tevita Cavubati is yellow-carded; there's patient phase play in front of the Fijian posts. The ball comes back to Dan Biggar, who launches another one of his diagonals. This time it's Adams who gathers and scores. Dan adds the extras. 7-10.

Not long afterwards, Adams thinks he's over again, but is in touch. But – with another Fijian in the sin bin – he gets another chance, and takes it. It's been a breathless first half for the winger and the whole of Wales. 14-10 at half-time.

Will those points blunt the islanders' enthusiasm? Hardly. James Davies is the next to see yellow, for not rolling away. Fiji kick for the corner, drive for the line, and earn a penalty try after Jerome Garces adjudges Wales to have brought down the maul. 14-17. There's worse to come when Biggar collides, sickeningly, with Liam Williams under a high ball. For a few long moments he lies still, before, to everyone's relief, running off the field. He's replaced by Rhys Patchell, who again is influential: kicking a penalty before feeding Jonathan Davies on the left. The Lions centre fends off Volavola and slips a neat backhand pass to Adams: the Blues man is over for his hat trick.

Seven minutes later, with Welsh fitness starting to tell, Gareth Davies makes a break and puts Liam Williams through on the inside. Patchell's conversion makes it 29-17. It's enough. There's still time for some more bone-crunching Fijian hits, and both Adams and Jonathan Davies are off – like Biggar – with worrying-looking injuries, but Wales have survived, again.

"That was one of the most physical matches I've played," says Adams, the hat-trick hero, afterwards. "And some of the most difficult players I've had to try and stop, as well! But we're really happy with the bonus-point win, and we've come out relatively unscathed."

Despite the heavy strapping on his leg, he assures me he's just suffered heavy bruising, and should be fit for the next match.

"That was a really physical game," says a relieved Warren Gatland. "They've got some incredible individual athletes. But I thought we showed some unbelievable character to fight our way back into it. I thought we looked fit and strong out there, and there were some good defensive sets."

The news on Dan Biggar and Jonathan Davies is less clear. Biggar didn't undergo a Head Injury Assessment, says

Gatland. Rather, he was withdrawn straight away following his collision. He's not being considered to face Uruguay. Davies, who hurt his knee, will be assessed in due course. "Knees are funny things," says the coach. Let's hope it's not too serious. Losing the Lions centre – whose intervention was so important tonight – would be a big blow.

Later that evening, we're live from the square outside the hotel. The last stragglers of the boozy day are hanging round nearby. I tell Jonathan, the presenter in Cardiff, that Wales are now odds-on to top Pool D and face France in the quarter-final back in Oita on Sunday week. I also talk a little about Typhoon Hagebis, a superstorm heading for Japan from the Pacific Ocean and on course to hit Tokyo this weekend. It's rumoured that the game between France and England, scheduled for Yokohama on Saturday, might be moved or even called off. There'll be more news on that tomorrow.

On the pitch, Wales have weathered a storm of their own. Next, their World Cup voyage takes them south to Kumamoto, for their final pool match against Uruguay.

8

Kumamoto

10 October: On the Road Again

We pitch up bleary-eyed at Oita Station the next morning to find the trains are packed with fans heading down to Kumamoto for the next Wales game in just three days' time. There are no seats available until the 4 o'clock train. So we trundle back to the hotel, cursing the luggage, which we leave at reception until later this afternoon.

Holed up in a burger restaurant, we watch the comings and goings of protagonists from the day before. An enormous Fijian player walks past, calves like cannonballs, pushing a pram and with a diminutive wife in tow; a group of Wales fans, probably awaiting a train like us, drift by, basking in their team's status as Pool D champions-elect. As we're leaving the restaurant, Semi Radradra, Fijian winger and man of the match last night, comes in with his wife and child. I can't resist a selfie with Semi. What a player. It's been said before, but it bears repeating: there's no place in the world that produces as many natural rugby players as the South Sea Islands.

The weather's fine again here, but there's an epic storm out in the Pacific – Typhoon Hagebis – and the tournament organisers are being forced to take evasive action. It's announced today that Saturday's matches between New Zealand and Italy in Toyota, and England and France in Yokohama, are to be cancelled on safety grounds, with the games being declared 0-0 draws and two points being awarded to each side. Sunday's Japan v. Scotland game, also due to be played at Yokohama, and Namibia v. Canada in Kamaishi are both on for now, but final decisions will be made on Sunday morning after the typhoon has passed.

This announcement is not likely to go down well with the Scots. They have to win well on Sunday night to progress to the quarter-finals, most likely at Japan's expense. England and France are both already through, so may welcome the break, although two weeks without a match going into the last eight could prove a mixed blessing. And spare a thought for Italy, who, although almost certainly doomed to defeat against the All Blacks, will be denied the chance to finish their tournament on the pitch. It also means we've probably seen the last of two *Azurri* greats – Sergio Parisse and Leonardo Ghiraldini – on the international stage. Ghiraldini, who'd spent months in rehab following a knee injury, reportedly broke down in tears when he heard the news.

As for the ITV Wales team, we're fortunate to be heading to Kumamoto, the southernmost of all the World Cup venues, and safe from the ravages of Hagebis. At one stage last week, it looked like the typhoon was headed our way: now it's changed direction and is on course to hit central Japan instead. And even by the standards of a country that experiences powerful typhoons on a regular basis, it looks like a monster, threatening winds of 130 mph and 30 inches of rain in affected areas.

By the time we get to Kumamoto, darkness has fallen. We head to the hotel, and adjourn to the restaurant for pizza. At the next table, there's a group of Welsh women who we quickly establish to be wives and girlfriends (and the odd mother-in-law, perhaps) of the players. There is also a smattering of fans, leaving to explore the city's nightlife. This time, it seems, there'll be no waiting for the entourage to arrive.

After the long wait for Fiji, we're on an accelerated timetable: the team to take on Uruguay will be announced tomorrow, and we're expecting plenty of changes.

11 October: Hanging round the barber shop

Gatland always said he'd use this game to rest his key men and give outsiders a chance, and he's proved as good as his word. There are 13 changes in the Wales side to take on *Los Teros*, with first starts in Japan for the likes of Hallam Amos, Ryan Elias, Adam Beard, Bradley Davies and Aled Davies. Justin Tipuric captains the side, for the first time, from the openside flank. Josh Adams has recovered from his dead leg well enough to start a third game on the left wing. There's still no definitive news on Dan Biggar and Jonathan Davies, but there seems cautious optimism around each. On my way back from the team announcement press conference I bump into Biggar in the lift, and he seems sharp and alert.

During the press conference, Gatland told the media that this game was definitely a chance for players to put their hands up for selection for the quarter-finals. After he's finished speaking, I spend twenty minutes with a man who probably doesn't need to put his hand up. Rhys Patchell has already impressed everyone with his 'super-sub' performances against Australia and Fiji. Now he gets the chance to start on Sunday. All along, he's been a picture of calm assurance, despite an injury-plagued last season which left him all but certain to miss out on the World Cup, had it not been for the untimely injury to Gareth Anscombe.

"It was a frustrating year, though not quite the disaster people made it out to be," Patchell tells me, as we chat on a sun-drenched patio at the team hotel. A wedding chapel, surreally, is just behind us.

"There's a feel for the game at outside half, and it's very difficult when you keep spending time on the touchline to regain that rhythm particularly quickly. I've learned over the years that rugby moves very quickly, and the longer you stick around a barber shop, the more chance you've got of getting a haircut. Here I am, and what a fortunate position I'm in."

I ask him how important it is to be resilient in his line of work. After all, he wears the number 10 jersey, which has an almost mythical quality in Wales.

"If you want to play there, you've got to have rhino skin. If the team goes well, inevitably the 10 gets a pat on the back. If the team goes poorly, inevitably you're in the firing line. That's how it is and that's how it'll always be."

"When you sit on the bench, you've got to be prepared for whatever the situation is. It's no good for the team if whoever comes on looks flustered. You want to portray a sense of calm, of 'I've got this'– even if you're a bit like a swan, looking like you're not doing much on top but paddling like mad underneath!"

At half-time in the Australia game, there was a nice moment where Dan Biggar, the man Patchell replaced after Biggar failed a Head Injury Assessment, was seen encouraging Patchell as the players left the pitch. The relationship between the two outside halves is clearly a supportive one.

"We both have an appreciation of how..." – he pauses to find the right word – "*fickle* rugby is. I think everyone here knows that if we want to go deep in this competition, it's going to be a squad effort. Dan's done phenomenally well when he's been on the field. It's been unfortunate for him that he's taken a couple of bumps. But he's been excellent with me, making sure I'm across everything – as has Jenks [skills coach Neil Jenkins], Steve [attack coach Stephen Jones], and the rest of the coaching staff."

Again, there's that sense of cohesion in the squad. A feeling more akin to a club team than a national side. Later, at training, I spend as much time watching the players who aren't taking part as those who are. Some are working hard on exercise bikes. Others watch on from the sidelines. Jonathan Davies is wearing some kind of compression sock on his left leg, but is walking without a limp and seems happy. Surely, if the news was really bad, we'd have heard by now.

Off the field, the mood is uglier. Some have endorsed the decision to cancel Saturday's matches on safety grounds, with New Zealand coach Steve Hansen calling the move "a no brainer". Others have questioned the contingencies put in place by the powers that be. Italian legend Sergio Parisse, whose World Cup days now appear to be behind him, wanted to know why Italy's game with the All Blacks wasn't moved to another date, and suggested the decision may have been different had it been New Zealand, not Italy, who needed the points to progress to the quarter-finals.

And the Scottish Rugby Union, alarmed by the prospect that their vital match against Japan in Yokohama on Sunday may also fall victim to the weather, have threatened the tournament organisers with legal action if the game isn't played. "For World Rugby to simply state that the game has to be cancelled goes against the whole sporting integrity of the tournament," said Mark Dodson, Chief Executive of Scottish Rugby. World Rugby have called Dodson's comments "disappointing" and pointed out that the Scots, in common with the other 19 teams, have signed a participation agreement stating that pool matches cannot be postponed. One possibility is that the match will be played behind closed doors, an outcome which would negate Japan's home advantage.

It's easy to sympathise with the Scottish position. Four years after a controversial refereeing decision saw them lose a World Cup quarter-final against Australia, to be sent home in these circumstances would be difficult to take. But it's hard to see what the organisers can do. Having taken the decision to cancel tomorrow's matches, they can't now be seen to be treating Japan v. Scotland differently. Some will say all the games should have been moved: at one point, it seems, that was considered. But World Rugby say the "sheer scale" of the typhoon, and the complexity of moving all the teams, meant the safety risks were too great. And, understandable though their frustration may be, I think the Scots need to be careful with their rhetoric: to be seen worrying about sporting prospects at a time when lives are at serious risk seems insensitive.

There's plenty to chew over as I head out to meet with a journalist friend in one of Kumamoto's busy arcades. Later, reunited with the others, we find ourselves in a *bierkeller*-style bar with Stan and Sharon, some Wales fans we met in Oita the other week, together with their daughter Rachael and son-in-law Ibuki. Ibuki is Japanese, and with his help, the family have been having a great time touring the country. He points out that there's a two-hour-long 'all you can drink' deal available. Later, we all move on to Celts, the inevitable Irish bar, where the festivities continue. The Welsh are out in force, the singing stretches into the night, and the typhoon seems mercifully far away.

12 October: From Kumamoto to Kentucky

We may be outside the area set to be affected by Hagebis, but today even here skies are grey and winds are gusty. I record a piece to camera for TV in the Kumamoto fanzone. An inspection of the venues for tomorrow's games, including the stadium in Yokohama, will be made tomorrow morning, local time. For the Scots, then, an anxious few hours lie ahead.

Ireland, playing Samoa in nearby Fukuoka, had – like Wales – been in the typhoon's firing line before it tracked east. Now their game this evening is going ahead, with the Irish needing to win to make sure of their place in the last eight. We gather in the fanzone to watch the match, surrounded by familiar faces from our travels around Japan. Ireland, with their forward-oriented game, prove too strong and they defeat Samoa 47-5, despite Irish centre Bundee Aki being red-carded in the first half for a high tackle. It's the seventh sending off of the tournament, three more already than in any other World Cup.

After we've eaten, we seek out a place mentioned in my guidebook: Good Time Charlie, a country music bar. It's run by a guy named Charlie Nagatani, aged in his 80s and described in the book as a 'living legend' of Japanese country music. Over beers, we sit and watch Charlie and his Japanese band, The Western Cannonballs, play songs straight out of the American south. In front of the stage, an entourage of older Japanese men and women, dressed in cowboy-style clothes and hats, line dance to the music. Not for the first time here, I feel like I've stepped into a David Lynch film. In the low light, surrounded by over 40 years'-worth of country and western memorabilia (and a photo of Charlie with Bill Clinton), the star of the show performs his signature song, 'Good Time Charlie', to an appreciative audience of mostly Welsh visitors.

From Kumamoto to Kentucky, Tokyo to Tennessee
I dreamed one day I'd sing and play the Grand Ole Opry
It's all I've ever wanted, all I've ever known
My name is Good Time Charlie, and I play that country gold.

Afterwards, Charlie, looking very sprightly at 83, walks around and shakes everyone's hand. We leave suffused with a warm glow, wowed once again by the enthusiasms of this strange country.

Back at the hotel, I turn on the TV to see the first pictures of the damage wrought by Typhoon Hagebis. The screen is filled by pictures of flooded streets, interspersed with solemn-looking news presenters. Journalist colleagues in Tokyo are all on lockdown in their hotels, advised not to venture outdoors. But this storm of storms has already claimed a couple of lives, and one wonders what the night holds for ordinary folk living outside the big cities.

13 October: Game day

Morning dawns gloriously in Kumamoto, but it's been grim in central Japan and there's been further loss of life overnight, though the exact death toll is not yet clear. In the circumstances, it seems wrong to be worrying about the fate of a rugby match, but breakfast is abuzz with talk about the Japan-Scotland game and whether it will happen or not. All the reports are of sunny skies over Yokohama, but until the stadium there has been inspected, we can't know for sure.

As luck would have it, WRU Chairman and World Rugby representative Gareth Davies is staying in our hotel, and can confirm to us that, though Canada v. Namibia – due to be played in Iwate Prefecture – has been cancelled, the Scotland game is in fact going ahead. Apparently, it wasn't so much a question of ensuring the pitch was playable, but rather making certain that the stadium staff, many of whom live in homes damaged by the typhoon, would be able to get to the venue to put the game on.

There are no issues on that front here, thankfully, and there's the usual kaleidoscope of colour, mostly red, as I make my way through the fanzone to meet the press bus going to the ground. It never ceases to amaze me how many Welsh people follow their teams abroad, no matter how far-flung the destination. We're not exactly an affluent country, so presumably many must save for years.

At the stadium, we're led to our seats by a colleague from ITV Sport, and it's another of those 'pinch me' moments: to get to where we're going, we walk around the edge of the playing bowl as the players warm up on the pitch in front of an expectant crowd. It's another glorious evening for rugby: cool and dry, the green mountains of central Kyushu rolling into the distance.

There's an odd moment in the lift on the way up to the media seats. I notice that the number 4 is omitted from the buttons. Instead, they go: 1, 2, 3, 5. It's an example of Japanese superstition about numbers – in this case specifically, tetraphobia: fear of the number 4. In Japanese, *shi*, the word for four, has exactly the same pronunciation as the word for death. For that reason, the fourth floor is often skipped in buildings, and the number is left out of phone numbers, business cards and home addresses.

I'm not superstitious, but it certainly seems that this game has been tainted by ill-fortune. It certainly doesn't live up to the drama of the last two. In fact, it's a fairly spectacular anti-climax.

Wales look by far the better side, but for 15 minutes they don't have any points to show for it. It looks like Hallam Amos has scored, but there's a forward pass. Nicky Smith eventually does cross, from close quarters, and Leigh Halfpenny converts. But that's that from Wales for the half. Uruguay, *Los Teros*, bottom of the pool and homeward-bound next week, kick two penalties. 7-6 at half-time.

The trouble is, it's not even as if there's an upset on the cards. You know Wales will pull clear – they're too good not to. But you also suspect, with a sort of weary resignation, that there won't be much to write home about when they do. It's that sort of game: a dead rubber for one team, a shot to nothing for the other, with a set of players trying too hard to impress. Within the first ten minutes of the second half, Patchell kicks for the corner and Wales edge forward. Eventually the ball comes back and it's spun wide to Josh Adams, who's in for his fifth try of the tournament. That's one short of the Wales World Cup record set by Shane Williams in 2007. Halfpenny adds the extras.

But we're still making hard work of it. Amos is over again ten minutes later, but from another forward pass. Halfpenny is visibly annoyed. Eventually, the Uruguayan number 7 is sin-binned, punishment for too many infringements by his team. Soon, the referee awards Wales a penalty try, after the Uruguayans collapse a maul. I'm just ready for the game to end. So are the crowd, who are in full Mexican-wave mood. You never get Mexican waves at good games.

Uruguay score a try next, via a chap sporting an impressive moustache-and-mullet combination, named German Kessler.

But the lead never looks in serious danger. Wales rouse themselves to score another two: the first from replacement Tomos Williams following a Halfpenny break; the second from Gareth Davies, another scrum half – this one a fine solo effort from a quick-tap penalty. It's also the last move of the game, and sews up a 35-13, bonus-point win, which somehow feels disappointing. At least the Japan game's on later.

The players and management go through their post-match media duties. Gatland says Wales didn't give Uruguay "enough respect" in the first half, Patchell admits they turned the ball over "too cheaply". In truth, I suspect they're glad to get this one out of the way. Few players have enhanced their selection prospects. Perhaps the quote of the night comes from a fan interviewed by Tom and Siân outside the stadium: "I'm happy, but there'll be some very embarrassed people in that Welsh squad tomorrow. I hope someone has a few words with them to explain some basics of what they need to do."

We shouldn't be too harsh. Wales did do what they needed to do. They've finished top of a World Cup pool for the first time since 1999, and have gone through the preliminary stages unbeaten for only the second time (the previous occasion being in 1987). They will face France – as opposed to England – in a winnable-looking quarter-final, and they have no fresh injury concerns. If you'd offered them all of that in Tokyo a month ago, they'd have snapped your arm off.

Shane Williams, a man all too well acquainted with the vicissitudes of top-flight sport, toes a diplomatic line:

"They got the job done, but it wasn't a perfect display from Wales. Very disjointed, very lateral in attack and very lethargic at the start of the game. However, if you win the match with a bonus point, you've got to be quite happy with the result."

And he's pleased with the prospect of a last-eight match against France, after *Les Bleus* broke Welsh hearts by beating them in the semi-final eight years ago.

"I was looking forward to a match-up with France again after 2011 – that one still stings for me, really. It'll be nice for the lads to get a bit of revenge after that one! France on their day are world beaters: Wales know that, and they'll have to give it their best."

But spare a thought for Hallam Amos, one of tonight's wingers, who but for some forward passes might have improved his international try-scoring account dramatically. In fact, he might have got a hat trick: his third try went begging when he dropped the ball in the act of diving for the line. Off air, I seek some insight into what went wrong from Shane, Wales' record try-scorer: "A brain fart," he says.

I suppose some things are just hard to explain.

We start our edit in the press room, with the Japan v. Scotland game on TV. It's everything the Wales match wasn't: a pulsating encounter between two sides with everything on the line in this tournament. Scotland score first, but the home team come storming back with three excellent first-half tries and another after the break. We miss the second half as we're on the bus coming back to Kumamoto, but we soon hear about the final score: 28-21 to Japan. In town, the fanzone is alive with overjoyed supporters. On the stage, a singer leads a chorus of something in Japanese, set to John Denver's 'Take Me Home, Country Roads'.

It's the first time – ever – that the Brave Blossoms have reached the knockout stages. They've done it in style, with four wins from four. And, of course, it's impossible to overlook the emotional context: the death toll from Hagebis still isn't clear, but it's rising. Tonight, after a minute's silence on the pitch, the players had a chance to lift the nation's mood. Judging by the celebratory scenes in this corner of Kyushu, they've succeeded, and in style.

The fanzone closes with a montage of memorable moments from the pool stages. With four intriguing quarter-finals in store, there should be many more to come.

9

Oita again

14 October: Baggage handlers

It's been a short stay in Kumamoto, and now we're back
off to Oita for Wales' quarter-final match with France on
Sunday. This means another train journey, via Kokura, on
the less swanky southern trains. It also means another ordeal
with the bags. This, I pledge, will be the last time. If we get
through to the semi-finals, we'll pay to have them shipped to
Tokyo. For now, though, it's frayed tempers all round as the
four of us struggle to get various unwieldy bits of camera kit,
plus bulging suitcases, on and off one train and onto another.
So far, we've been organised when changing trains, so have
managed not to leave any kit on board. But there's a hairy
moment today when we dash from one train to another,
before noticing we're without Siân. Thankfully, she's made
it onto the train, but has to fight her way through several
carriages to find us, dragging her heavy kit behind her.

Still, spending a little time reading about the aftermath
of Hagebis puts our problems into perspective. The latest
estimate puts the death toll from the typhoon at 56, with
16 missing and around 38,000 displaced from their homes
amidst flooding and landslides. It's also humbling to learn

of the efforts that went into ensuring the Japan v. Scotland game went ahead. Reportedly, officials slept in the stadium at Yokohama on Saturday night, so they could start assessing the damage at dawn. Getting the transport networks up and running for thousands of fans and staff must have been a logistical nightmare. But the organisers made it happen, and were rewarded with an unforgettable evening. It seems TV viewers agreed: it's claimed the game drew a peak audience of more than half the Japanese population – 60 million people.

In Oita, we settle into our hotel (which, I'm pleased to say, has a very nice *onsen*), and head out for a steak dinner. The weather's much cooler up here, and so far, there are no fans to be seen. Presumably they're all hitting the tourist trail up country before the big weekend.

16 October: Magic in the air

There may be few fans here, but there are plenty of pundits. Yesterday I bumped into Eddie Butler, here to commentate on Sunday's game for the host broadcaster. Eddie fancies Wales to win, and makes England marginal favourites to defeat Australia. Recent history would suggest he's right about both games. England have had the advantage over the Wallabies in recent seasons, and Wales have won seven of their last eight against France.

And in the camp, the signs are positive. Wales say they have a clean bill of health ahead of the match, with Jonathan Davies (knee), Dan Biggar (concussion), and George North (ankle) all back in training. It makes for quite a contrast with the state the squad found themselves in at the 2015 World Cup in England.

"Obviously four years ago we had a tough run of injuries during the pool stages and before," says hooker Ken Owens. "So it's been great that everyone's come through unscathed and we're in a good position."

One theme of the week is sure to be the last (and so far, only) time Wales met France at the World Cup, back in 2011. That occasion, of course, saw Warren Gatland's men beaten by a point in the semi-final, after captain Sam Warburton was sent off. Yesterday, attack coach Stephen Jones (who played that night) said that the experience would be "fuel" to the current crop of players. Today, Neil Jenkins, part of the coaching team eight years ago, seems a little less convinced:

"At the end of the day it's another game on Sunday – a totally different game. I'm not sure if what's gone [before] makes too much of a difference. There's a lot at stake and we'll need to be ready, that's for sure."

With only four survivors from that fateful night in the current squad, I'm not sure if Auckland will be motivation for the players. But I think it will be for the coaches, who were all involved back then. Whatever, Jenkins says he expects a tough outing against a French side who have had an extra week's rest because of the typhoon.

"It was a bit disappointing from our point of view not to see what would have gone on in the England game [France's opponents in the cancelled match]. But I have no doubt that they'll be ready to go on Sunday. They've got some fantastic players and I'm sure they'll play well."

After the press conference, we film training near the team's hotel in Beppu. The weather's glorious, and we lie on the grass waiting for the players to appear. In the taxi back to the station, the white-gloved driver hands out sweets. It's the second piece of kindness I've encountered in the last few days. At Kumamoto Station, a cashier ran after me with an item that I'd dropped, despite having a queue of people to deal with. Japanese *omotenashi* (roughly translated, 'hospitality') is alive and well.

Back in Oita, we head out to get some pictures of the city. First, we head to the castle, which is little more than a ruin, but still impressive by night. The remains of a tower, hidden by day behind scaffolding, are lit up by thousands of bulbs to give a ghostly impression of how it once appeared. Inside the castle ramparts, there's a collection of *nebuta* – carnival floats in the form of giant lanterns made of *washi* paper – featuring fantastical figures from Japanese mythology and rugby. One depicts a samurai swordsman; another an ogre-like figure in a white jersey with glowing slits for eyes, kicking a rugby ball. Perhaps he's supposed to be English. Lit up by bulbs from inside, they stand out impressively in the dark. Ambient music gently fills the air.

I head back to the hotel to collect some kit. Oita City is not in any of our guidebooks: I suppose it lacks the martial history of Kumamoto with its castle, or the hot springs and seaside resort appeal of nearby Beppu. But there's something beautiful about it tonight; the murals in the underpass, the mist gently rising from the ground in the plaza by the station (another art installation), the fairy lights in the trees. I'm not sure how the infrastructure here will cope with four sets of thirsty rugby fans (England and Australia also play in Oita on Saturday), but to stroll the streets of the city on a mild autumn night is pleasant indeed.

Tonight's dinner is a treat, too. It's called *okonomiyaki* – literally, 'as you like it' – and is a sort of many-layered pancake. This particular one originated in Hiroshima, and its ingredients include bacon, eggs and *yakisoba* noodles. The four of us sit at the counter while the chef works his magic on the iron hotplate in front of us. Apparently, *okonomiyaki* became popular in Hiroshima when rice was scarce in the years following the Second World War, and has remained a favourite ever since. As we tuck in, relishing the different flavours and sweet brown sauce (very like the Worcestershire variety back home), it's easy to see why.

17 October: Winter Wonderland

Today's a day off, so this afternoon Tom and I head back to Beppu to try out one of the larger *onsen* there. We make for the Suginoi Hotel, which, it seems, is halfway up a mountain. Here there's a big, outdoor unisex bath that permits the wearing of swimming costumes. Last time Wales were in Beppu, they stayed in this hotel. This week, it's home to the England team.

We head outside and immerse ourselves in the warm water, which is pumped into pools large enough to swim in (although you'll soon get uncomfortably hot if you try). The bathers are mostly Japanese, including families with small children, though there are some westerners. I get chatting to a

Frenchman who happens to be a World Rugby representative. Flatteringly, he asks me if I'm a player, before bemoaning how 'professional' the game has become. He preferred the amateur days, when players had jobs outside the game, and rugby was a hobby rather than an occupation.

I pause to take in the surrounding scenery. As Tom points out, it's almost Jurassic, with steam rising from a hundred hot springs in the surrounding hillsides. As dusk falls, city lights twinkle into life below us. Before we leave, I spend a blissful half hour in the flotation pool, which is housed in a conical building next to the baths. I float in the salty water – saline enough to keep me buoyant – my ears beneath the surface so I can listen to restful music piped through underwater speakers. As I pass beneath the aperture in the top of the building, droplets of rain fall gently onto my face. At this moment, our struggles with the bags seem far away.

It's an odd place, mind, this hotel. After we leave the *onsen*, we pass through an arcade where Japanese holidaymakers, many clad in bathrobes, are enjoying the games. The escalators down to the lobby are flanked by Christmas trees, and outside there are illuminated figures of Father Christmas, a snowman and reindeer. In this mountain setting, you could easily imagine you were in some kind of weird ski resort.

Once again, I feel somewhat disoriented, as must the England players who we see around the place. A group including Jamie George and Elliot Daly sit in the arcade playing on the claw crane (that machine where you attempt to pick up cuddly toys using a remote-controlled grabber). In the lobby, Joe Marler and Joe Launchbury stride past. Today

Eddie Jones, the England coach, named his team to take on Australia on Saturday. Tomorrow it's Wales' turn.

We stop for a drink near Beppu Station, and find ourselves sitting next to a large group of England fans. After the midweek lull, it feels like the mood is changing. Back in Oita, we pass a quiet evening, readying ourselves for the busy days ahead.

18 October: Under the radar

It's knockout rugby, and the time for experimentation is over. Today Warren Gatland named the same starting XV that did so well against Australia in Tokyo. The only changes to the 23 from that day are among the replacements, where Adam Beard is preferred to Aaron Shingler, Rhys Carré gets the nod over Nicky Smith, and Leigh Halfpenny is rewarded for his man-of-the-match showing against Uruguay, at the expense of Owen Watkin.

Pleasingly, Gatland says centres Jonathan Davies and Hadleigh Parkes (who's had a shoulder problem) have come through training and are ready to play. Dan Biggar is restored to the number 10 jersey, though in their press release, Wales were keen to stress that he'd only been selected after passing an MRI scan and having two separate meetings with a consultant. "Player welfare," says the statement, "is independent of any team or competition." It's not surprising they've been so diligent. In the last few years, America's NFL has paid out millions of dollars in compensation to players affected in later life by concussion sustained when playing. It's an issue that's never been more relevant.

As for the game itself, the Wales coach says his team have the self-confidence to be comfortable with their tag as favourites: "If you take out the World Cup warm up-games, we've won 18 competitive games in a row. We're Grand Slam champions – we know as we go on in tournaments, we get stronger and more confident and cohesive as a unit, and we just think we're building nicely."

That said, he still thinks that Wales are considered outsiders when it comes to winning the competition: "We still feel we're going in under the radar. There's a lot more emphasis and talk about other teams and other games and that suits us. But there's a lot of belief and self-confidence within our group."

Against Australia, Wales took the Wallabies by surprise with a drop goal just minutes into the game, clearly a strategy to get early points on the board. And it seems there might be some new tactics this time, designed especially with the French in mind.

"You've got to bring things that teams aren't expecting. We felt we did that in the Six Nations with the way we played against Ireland and England. We're aware of France's individual threats: they're a big side with an offloading game. But they're the team that have had the most turnovers in this competition and they've played one game fewer. So there are potentially opportunities there from turnover situations."

And there's a nod to the Six Nations match of 2019, when Wales pounced on French mistakes to overhaul a 16-0 half-time deficit: "For us, playing France is often about lost causes. Four of our last seven tries have been about situations where we've kept working hard to chase and one of their players has made an error and we've capitalised on it. Shaun [Edwards] has been a little bit more pumped up this week. We've been working hard defensively. He wasn't too happy about conceding a try against Uruguay and let the players know pretty clearly in the changing room afterwards. We've prepared extremely well, and we're going into this game with a lot of confidence."

At 22, Aaron Wainwright will be the youngest player in the starting XV (although Carré, on the bench, is younger at 21). Five years ago, Wainwright was playing football with Cardiff City's academy. Now he's preparing for a Rugby World Cup quarter-final.

"It's been a long couple of years. To be playing in a quarter-final is massive. I didn't think it would go this far. I started playing with my mates in school and it just carried on from there. I'm really excited and ready to go on the weekend."

Wainwright's rise, via Whiteheads RFC in Newport and Cardiff Met, reminds me of the emergence of Dan Lydiate and Sam Warburton in 2011. Now, as then, a little-known Welsh flanker is making a name for himself on the biggest stage.

In Oita, the atmosphere is much livelier now we're on the eve of the big weekend. English, Australian, Welsh and French fans mingle good naturedly in the fanzones and the pop-up bar in front of the station. "They [the French team] are all over the shop, aren't they?" says one Welsh supporter. "They only play for 40 minutes. We'll play for the full 80. I reckon there'll be 15 points in it." "We are not the favourites," admits a Frenchman nearby, "but I think this is why we will win." Being French, there's a total logic in what he says: there are few more dangerous beasts in sport than unfancied French rugby teams. No one's more adept at upsetting the form book, as we saw in 1999 and 2007, when *Les Bleus* famously shocked the All Blacks. In recent years, that volatile genius has lain dormant... let's hope it doesn't spark into life on Sunday.

19 October: And then there were six

Then again, there aren't many French greats of yesteryear that can boast as good a World Cup try-scoring record as one of our very own current Welsh crop. Winger Josh Adams took his tally to five when he crossed against Uruguay last week. That's joint top (along with Japan's Kotaro Matsushima) of the tournament try-scoring chart, and only one short of Shane Williams' record for Wales at a World Cup.

"I haven't heard from Shane," smiles Josh at today's eve-of-match press conference. "Now I know I'm one behind him, it would be good if I could level with him – or even overtake him, hopefully."

A try-scorer against France in February during Wales' Six Nations great escape, Adams acknowledges how important it will be not to let the French get off to another strong start.

"They came out of the blocks well, and we found ourselves 16 points behind at half-time. We definitely need to start well if we want to build into the game better," he says, before echoing Gatland's words yesterday about the quiet confidence in the camp. "It's important we approach the week like we do any other. It's been slowly building this week... there's been a bit of a spike in training – I'm sure the forwards can vouch for that! It's relaxed; there's been a good mood with everyone. And none of us are ready to go home."

Four teams will be going home after this weekend, however, whether they like it or not, and today we find out the identity of two of them. First up, it's England v. Australia. And although the Wallabies fight back after a strong English start to make it 17-16 early in the second half, Eddie Jones' men pull away impressively, cantering to a comprehensive 40-16 victory. It's an even more one-sided affair in the evening match in Yokohama, where New Zealand make short work of a wretched Irish side. 22-0 at half-time, there's little to write home about from the Irish after the break, and they eventually go down to a 46-14 defeat. It's a dramatic fall from grace for the team who reached number 1 in the world this year, and who have beaten the All Blacks twice since 2016. And it's also a sad end for Joe Schmidt, the architect of that rise up the rankings, who quits as coach after this tournament.

As we watch the action in the Oita fanzone, England and Australia fans return from their match in varying states of morale (and inebriation). We've met up with our boss – who's making a flying visit to Japan for quarter-final weekend – and are ourselves doing valiant work on the drinking front. After we leave the fanzone, we get caught up in an impromptu arm-wrestling and limbo-dancing competition with some England supporters. It's all good fun.

Schmidt, of course, won't be the only coach hanging up his spurs when the World Cup ends. Warren Gatland is also just one loss away from the end of the road. All week, players and coaches have been saying they're not ready to head home, and that they want to keep their boss' tenure going for another few games. Win tomorrow, and they know they'll be here till the end of the tournament – be that for the final or the bronze final. Can they do it? We're about to find out.

20 October: That was close

"I'm nervous at the fact we're not nervous," says a colleague of mine on her Twitter feed this afternoon (or morning, back in Wales) – which, thinking about it, is a good observation. All week we've been in this bubble of confidence, it seems, trotting out our seven-from-eight-wins statistics and buying into the narrative about the flaky French. I think I've been overconfident – complacent, even. Let's hope to God the players haven't.

And there's bad news before the game. Jonathan Davies, who's been nursing that knee injury, has withdrawn from the team. Given the amount of strapping around his left leg this week, many were sceptical about his chances, and their fears have been realised. Owen Watkin, Jonathan's replacement, is a promising young player, but Wales are now shorn of one of their main attacking threats.

Still, in the first few moments, all seems well. France fumble the ball from the kick-off, and Wales go through the phases, probing for an opening. But a Biggar up-and-under goes long, Maxime Médard calls a mark, and soon France are off on a raid down Wales' right. George North scrambles back after a kick, with Yoann Huget in hot pursuit, and the danger is averted. But France have possession again and are looking menacing. The Welsh defends holds, and holds, until it can hold no longer. Sébastien Vahaamahina, the giant lock, is over for the game's first try. Romain Ntamack misses a straightforward conversion, but it's 0-5 to France.

It's a sobering moment. But it's about to get worse. From the kick-off, *Les Bleus* work the ball left. Virimi Vakatawa, the fleet-footed centre, leaves Navidi for dead in midfield. The ball goes inside, and inside again, and it's openside Charles Ollivon, with no red shirts in front of him, who has the pace to finish under the posts. Ntamack can't miss this conversion, and it's 0-12.

For a second time at this World Cup, Wales find themselves two tries down after 10 minutes. But this time they're against a Tier 1 nation who – their Paris implosion in 2019 notwithstanding – should have the nous to defend their lead. For all the talk of them being undercooked after their two-week break, France look the fitter and fresher of the sides.

As against Fiji, though, Wales score next. Jake Ball puts in a big hit on Guilhem Guirado, the French skipper, who spills the ball into the path of Aaron Wainwright. The former midfielder shows a turn of speed straight off the soccer pitch to sprint home. Biggar converts, and Wales are back in it.

Biggar kicks another penalty, and it's a two-point game, but then there's another setback for Wales. Ross Moriarty – on for Navidi, who's limped off with a worrying-looking injury – goes high on Gaël Fickou. Referee Jaco Peyper shows him a yellow card. France take full advantage: Vakatawa, who's having a great game, scores a try of his own against the outnumbered Welsh defence.

Soon after that, France have the chance to kick for the corner, but opt to go for goal: fortunately for Wales, Ntamack misses. But it's still 10-19 at half-time. The inspired French team we worried about has turned up. As it stands, I can't see a way back.

But big games turn on small moments. In this case, it's a rather unsavoury one. On 49 minutes, and with France once again threatening the Welsh line, Peyper blows his whistle for an infringement at a maul. But wait: the television match official has spotted something. 40-odd thousand people crane their necks to watch the big-screen replay. Vahaamahina, hero of the first half, becomes annoyed at the attentions of Wainwright... and elbows him, hard and deliberately, in the jaw. It's a clear red card, and that's what the referee gives. Nine years after Auckland, this time it's a French player being given his marching orders. Unlike Auckland, there can be no debate about it.

When Biggar kicks another penalty, I wonder if Wales are closing in. But they're finding it hard to make the decisive breakthrough. In fact, France look the more likely, and come close to scoring in the corner. When, with less than 10 minutes left, Wales knock the ball on in the shadow of the French posts, the three of us are contemplating our flight home. But there's one more chance: France have a put-in at a scrum near their line. Wales, complete with replacement front row, summon a huge shove. Tomos Williams rips the ball from Ollivon, Justin Tipuric gathers and is tackled just short. The ball comes back, Ross Moriarty drives for the line, and scores.

Biggar converts, and finally, the French resistance is broken. When he kicks the ball high into the stand after 80 minutes, there are sighs of relief from Oita to Ogmore Vale. Somehow, again, Wales have done it: they're in the World Cup semi-final for only the third time.

"I think relief is the overriding emotion in the dressing room at the moment," says the Wales outside half afterwards. "We probably weren't the most skilful team in the quarter-finals this weekend, but we've got as much fight and character as any of them, and that'll stand us in great stead for the semi-final next week."

"The message at half-time was that we've got to score next," says Warren Gatland, who reveals he was preparing his farewell speech in the coaches' box. "We were able to do that. The red card was obviously pretty significant. But the thing I'm proud of is that the guys didn't give in. Not the prettiest in the world, but some great character shown."

For Sam Warburton, watching on from the ITV Wales studio in Cardiff, sympathy for the dismissed Vahaamahina is in short supply: "It was a disgrace. Wainwright's within his rights to go through that maul and try and get his hands on the ball. And to get an elbow in the face – that could have fractured or dislocated his jaw. The fact he had a red card was exactly the right result."

It's hard not to conclude that Vahaamahina has cost his team a spot in the World Cup semi-final. It's also hard not to notice the almost eerie symmetry with the 2011 game: a team reduced to 14 men loses by a point, despite having the better of the play. Eight years on, the score is settled.

As President Barack Obama once said (quoting a nineteenth-century preacher named Theodore Parker): "the arc of the moral universe is long, but it bends towards justice."

I do a piece to camera next to the now-deserted pitch, and we retreat to the media room to edit, keeping one eye on the evening's other quarter-final between South Africa and Japan. This time, it's a bridge too far for the Brave Blossoms: the physically more powerful Springboks eventually prevail 26-3. Afterwards, despite the traditional Japanese tendency to avoid displays of emotion in public at all costs, the Japan players are understandably and visibly gutted, with several in tears. This clearly meant a lot to them. And what a tournament they've had: deservedly reaching the knock-out stages for the first time ever, and playing with a rare verve and flair along the way. There are already calls for them to be added to the Rugby Championship. How practical that is, I'm not sure, but I hope they can use their success here to go onto bigger and better things. Rugby needs more competitive teams.

As for Wales, they've done it. Whatever happens, they – and we – will now be here until the end of the tournament. To reach the final, as opposed to the bronze final, they'll have to improve. But, as Biggar, Gatland, and no end of pundits have pointed out, one quality they certainly have is character. Alone, that won't be enough to win Wales the Webb Ellis Cup on 2 November. But it's not a bad start: and who's to say it can't carry them further yet?

10

Tokyo part 3

21 October: Room service

The station at Oita is heaving this morning, as four loads of
rugby fans move up country in one swarm. We pile onto the
train to Kokura, mercifully without some of the bags, which
we're having sent separately, but still heavily laden enough.
It's like a cattle train on board, with nowhere near enough
room for all the passengers. I'm lucky enough to find a seat;
others are forced to perch on top of suitcases or stand while
the train weaves from side to side on the twisting track north.

At Kokura, we change. The crowds are thinner on board
the next train, for Shin-Osaka, and thinner again as we make
our final connection, bound for Tokyo. As we speed silently
through Japan's main island, the daylight fading outside,
we don't talk much. We've been on the road for nearly six
weeks now, and we're starting to feel fatigued. Living out of
a suitcase, dragging kit from one place to another, too many
late nights – it's all beginning to take its toll.

I don't know whether it's my pessimistic state of mind,
but I'm struggling to see Wales winning on Sunday. They
were outplayed yesterday, and are lucky to still be in the
competition. And this evening, there's news of another blow

to their chances: Josh Navidi, forced to limp off against France, has torn his hamstring and is out for the rest of the tournament. Wales will be calling for a replacement, but probably not in the back row: rather, with question marks still over Jonathan Davies and his knee, the coaches are considering summoning a midfield player – possibly Scott Williams, who missed out on selection for the original 31-man party.

Elsewhere, yesterday's ref Jaco Peyper is in hot water after a photo emerged of him posing with some Welsh fans. In it, they appear to be making an elbow gesture, presumably in reference to the incident which saw Sébastien Vahaamahina sent off. The French Rugby Union has not seen the funny side of this incident, and its vice president is demanding an explanation. World Rugby say they're investigating, and there's speculation that Peyper may be removed from refereeing duties for the rest of the World Cup. This, to my mind, would be an overreaction: I can't see how the image is anything other than a bit of fun.

In Tokyo, it's cooler than it was when we first stayed here over a month ago. Rain gently patters over the pedestrians packed onto the city's busy crossings. The seasons are changing. Back at the Shinjuku Hilton, our home for a third time on this trip, I work late into the evening. It's too late to go for dinner, and I'm not feeling sociable anyway. I order room service, a greasy club sandwich covered incongruously by a silver platter. Outside, the lights in the skyscraper office windows glow.

22 October: Case for the defence

Another grey day dawns over Tokyo. As we sit in a taxi on our way across town for today's press conference, the city traffic seems even busier than normal. We soon realise the reason why: today marks the enthronement of Emperor Naruhito, Japan's first new emperor for nearly 30 years. Foreign dignitaries from around the world are here to attend the ancient ceremony, including the Prince of Wales.

At the team hotel, our very own rugby royalty is beginning the build-up towards its biggest game in eight years. Earlier, it was confirmed that Blues winger Owen Lane – who was unfortunate not to make the squad in September – is on his way out to Japan to provide injury cover. Meanwhile, it's defence coach Shaun Edwards' turn to answer questions from the press. Yes, he says, he's disappointed with the defensive showing against France, but every cloud has a silver lining:

"I wasn't happy with the way we conceded those 19 points. We're struggling to stop teams on the goal line at the moment, like a lot of teams are. But I was very pleased that we scored 14 points from defence: an unbelievable rip from Tomos which set up the last try, and a big shot from Jake which dislodged the ball so we could score the first try. It's a bit similar to Australia really – we scored 10 points against them with defence."

Earlier in the campaign, Edwards said he'd be "unbelievably disappointed" if Wales didn't reach their second semi-final of the Gatland era. Now they're here, he says it's "seize the moment time".

"These opportunities don't come along very often. Last time was 2011: we just missed out then. You want to be in the big games and there's no bigger than the World Cup Final."

Assuming Jonathan Davies is fit (Edwards says he's progressing well), there'll most likely only be four survivors from that 2011 game in the starting team for Sunday. But does Wales' defensive guru think this is a better side than the one which played then?

"We're probably on a better run than we were back in 2011. It's a year and a half since we've lost a competitive game. So we've probably got a bit more confidence than we had then, belief in our game plan, belief in the way we play."

And listening to Dillon Lewis, who's next to appear in front of the cameras alongside front-row colleague Rhys Carré, the excitement over Sunday's game is palpable:

"It's definitely something we're all thinking about. Everyone in the team, including staff, can't wait for the game and for the opportunity for us to potentially play in a final."

But, waiting to film training at a chilly practice ground later that afternoon, the nagging doubts persist. Yes, Wales have won their last four matches against South Africa, including the most recent encounter 11 months ago; but that Springbok team looked very different to this one, and since then, they've won the Rugby Championship and seem far more like their old selves. And surely, to beat them, Wales will have to do more than simply engage in an 'arm wrestle' up front? The South African forwards have looked pretty formidable here so far.

At the World Cup megastore, we conduct a straw poll among fans we find doing a spot of afternoon shopping: who, from the four teams remaining, will reach the final on 2 November, and why?

"Let's hope it's not New Zealand, England or South Africa," says one Australian, ruefully, before conceding he can't see beyond a New Zealand v. South Africa final. "The All Blacks and the Welsh," says another Wallaby supporter, "and I think the All Blacks will win it." A Japanese lady plumps for New Zealand and Wales, too, but won't be drawn on a winner.

In our admittedly unscientific research, the Wales v. All Blacks option does seem a dream pairing. I must confess, the prospect of watching Wales bid to end their 66-year losing streak against the New Zealanders – AND win a World Cup in the process – is rather alluring.

After editing our piece for tonight's news, we head out for a drink in the Hub British bar, where Tom and I watched Japan shock Ireland last month. A Wales win over South Africa would not be a giant-killing on that scale, but for fans hoping to see their side reach its first ever World Cup Final, I suspect it would be met with even wilder celebrations.

24 October: The cheetah-racer

When you're looking for a South African perspective on the big game, who better to ask than a man so famous for his speed on the field of play that he once raced a cheetah? I'm talking about Bryan Habana, of course, the legendary Springbok winger, World Cup-winner, and joint tournament record try-scorer.

I meet Bryan on the roof terrace of a downtown restaurant, and am immediately struck by two things: his friendliness (he greets Tom and me with a wide grin and a warm handshake), and his size. He's not tall, but wide... as if carved from a block of South African granite.

He never lost to Wales. And he doesn't expect his successors in the Springbok shirt to lose either, despite the recent run of Welsh wins.

"I think South Africa under Rassie [coach 'Rassie' Erasmus], with how he plans tactically, is going to be very different to what we've seen previously. In 2018 in Washington [where Wales won 22-20], it was probably the second string of South African players who got the opportunity to play. Do I believe it'll be close? Without a doubt. Do I believe South Africa have the goods to pull through? Without a doubt as well."

It should certainly be close. In the last ten Wales v. South Africa matches, the winning margin has never been greater than 10 points. It's a far cry from the days where Welsh teams were easy meat for the 'Boks. Habana has been impressed.

"Under Warren Gatland, they've created a culture of winning. They won 14 games in a row. They've won Six Nations, they've won Grand Slams, and that becomes a little bit worrying from a South African perspective. Even though they perhaps slipped up pre-tournament in one or two games, they haven't lost that ability and experience to win."

Wales will need all that experience this weekend. The 'Boks have just won the Rugby Championship for the first time in ten years, drawing with New Zealand in the process. As ever, their success has been based on the brute strength of their forward pack: men like Eben Etzebeth, 'The Beast' Tendai Mtawarira and Duane Vermeulen. But, in Cheslin Kolbe and Makazole Mapimpi, they've also unearthed two dangerous wingers. As a former wide-man himself, Habana is relishing the contest between those two and the Welsh pair of Josh Adams and George North.

"Every time Mapimpi gets his hands on the ball, you feel he's going to score a try. And Cheslin Kolbe's probably run the most metres in the tournament so far. Josh Adams has an incredible game under the high ball, which really helps that Welsh defensive pattern and getting turnover ball. His ability to work off his wing, and find himself in positions to score tries, is one of the highlights of being a winger."

With five tries apiece at the tournament so far, Adams and Mapimpi are within striking distance of Habana's mark of eight tries at a World Cup (which he holds jointly with Jonah Lomu and Julian Savea). But neither Adams nor his Springbok counterpart has ever raced a cheetah, as Habana once did. The 'race', in 2007, was held to raise awareness of the threat posed to the species, and saw the player given a 50-metre head start. After today's interview, I ask him if he won. "No," comes the answer. "I'm just glad it didn't see my arse as a nice juicy rump steak."

*****

Whether Wales have been feasting on red meat in preparation for the big game is unclear, but they did have a royal visitor yesterday. The Prince of Wales – in town for the enthronement of Emperor Naruhito, as mentioned above – dropped by at training to meet the players. It was day to remember in particular for new arrival Owen Lane, who was presented with his World Cup cap by His Royal Highness:

"I was a bit cheeky this morning and asked him would he present a cap to Owen, and he said he would be absolutely delighted," said team manager Alan Phillips. "Every time you meet him, you are impressed by him as a person. He is very humble, a quiet man and nice company."

Back at our hotel in Shinjuku, there's been no shortage of rugby royalty. In addition to Bryan Habana, this week I've already spotted Gareth 'Alfie' Thomas and Mike Phillips – here to work on ITV's match coverage – and World Cup-winner Jonny Wilkinson. Former Lions captains Paul O'Connell and Martin Johnson are also here, while Tom spotted Brian O'Driscoll in the foyer.

We're about to reach the business end of rugby's biggest showpiece, and the game's biggest names are here to see it.

25 October: "When you want something badly enough..."

The South Africa game already appeared a daunting task. Today, it looks a little bit harder. Last night, reports emerged that Liam Williams was likely to miss the game after suffering an injury in training. Today, Wales confirmed the worst: Williams has damaged an ankle, and will sit out the rest of the tournament. As one of the side's leading lights in attack, the absence of the Lions full back will be a blow.

But Warren Gatland has a way of calming worried fans – and reporters – and, after confirming that Leigh Halfpenny ("probably the best defensive full back in the world") will start against the Springboks, offers this comforting take on the situation:

"To be honest, we had a long debate over whether we should start Leigh in the first place, and potentially move Liam to the wing. Obviously, we're disappointed for Liam, who's a world-class player. It's a change, but we don't think we're weakened in any way."

Outside, the weather is grimmer than the Wales coach's mood. It's teeming with rain, as Tokyo is battered by the remnants of another typhoon (this one, mercifully, never made landfall). Pedestrians battle through the elements, trying to hold onto their umbrellas. The forecast for the weekend is OK, but today's captains' runs at Yokohama Stadium – where all four semi-finalists are due to train – will be conducted ankle-deep in water.

Whether they're just putting a brave face on it, I don't know, but there seems no dampening the spirits of the Wales hierarchy. Both coach and captain project their usual air of flinty defiance from the top table at the team hotel. "At this stage of the tournament, you're always going to lose a couple of quality players," insists Gatland. He adds that those remaining are ready for their once-in-a-lifetime opportunity.

"In life, you get chances [like this] very rarely, and you have to take them with both hands. When you want something badly enough, when you really, really want it, it can happen. And we've got a group of players who really want to give a good performance on Sunday and hopefully get to the World Cup Final."

To do so, they'll have to overcome the odds. Despite their excellent recent record against the 'Boks, Wales are unfancied to beat them when it really counts. But Gatland insists he's more confident about this match than the preceding one against France, and is happy for the pundits to play down their chances.

"If they continue to do that, it'll be brilliant. Please, please, keep doing that. It does get us up when people write us off. I can't understand why people would write us off when our record against South Africa over the past four or five years has been pretty good."

As expected, Ross Moriarty comes into the back row in place of the injured Josh Navidi, with Aaron Shingler restored to the bench. Owen Watkin – fresh from the emergency appearance against France – is also among the replacements.

South Africa, too, have been affected by injury: winger Cheslin Kolbe – described by one reporter as "more slippery than a buttered otter" – is out with an ankle problem. Kolbe's absence might mean a marginally easier evening for his counterpart Josh Adams, and the in-form winger can't wait for his team's chance to make history.

"We've never reached a World Cup Final, and I think we've all got the feeling that this is the best opportunity we've had in a long time to do that. We're all pretty focused on making sure that this isn't our last competitive match. If we can reach the final, it's going to be something that lives on with every one of us in the squad."

"For every one of us, it's the biggest game of our careers so far," adds Gareth Davies, sitting alongside him. "The World Cup's been in the back of our minds for a long time now. We started the tournament pretty well but we still feel we've got another big performance in us. I don't think we've had one full 80-minute performance yet, and we know that we'll have to have that to come away with the win."

I hail a taxi and head back to the hotel through the driving rain. In reception, I bump into Shane Williams and Mike Phillips, and we go for coffee. Phillips seems to be enjoying his rugby academy business in Dubai, where he lives with his wife and baby son. Shane – who of course used to play in Japan – has had no shortage of events to keep himself busy in the six or so weeks he's been here. As far as the game's concerned, they both seem confident. Shane predicts Wales will "kick the arse" off the ball, which seems a good shout, especially against a side who, according to Gatland, put boot to ball 30 times in the quarter-final. In the pressure cooker of a World Cup semi-final, it seems unlikely that either team will abandon their tried-and-tested tactics. So, lots of kicking, lots of tackling, lots of grunt. Dull, perhaps: but if Wales win, who cares?

I return to my room to edit my piece for tonight's news. Later, with the rain finally abating, Tom and I head out on the hunt for Wales fans. They're few and far between: the ones we do find hover between confident and cautious. "We've got *hwyl*, and Gatland's got us right," says one. "If it's going to get won, it'll get won up front," says another. "We've got to make the first 40 minutes the biggest of our lives."

Later, we venture into Shinjuku to do our weekly 2 a.m. live slot for the news. Even at this late hour, work is being carried out on the streets: a crane lifts beams onto a building rooftop, branches are hacked back on an overgrown tree. In Tokyo, life, and work, never stops. As we line up for the broadcast, it strikes me that everyone we've spoken to – from Gatland, to the players, to the fans – is optimistic, or at least they're doing their best to sound that way. The presenter asks me if this feels like 2011, the last time Wales reached a World Cup semi-final. I answer that it seems different. Back then, we were strongly fancied to win the game; this time, despite the evidence of recent matches, we're not. But then, I add, things didn't turn out as expected in '11. Perhaps they won't this time, either.

Sometimes sport doesn't follow the script.

26 October: Awesome England

After yesterday's downpour, today the sun is shining in Tokyo. The weather is matched by the demeanour of Stephen Jones, Wales' forever bright and cheerful attack coach, who's on duty at the eve-of-match press conference. Jones, of course, never expected to be here. But after Rob Howley's untimely return to Wales, the Scarlets man was drafted in. Unlike the other coaches, for Jones this is a beginning, not an end. He'll be staying on to assist the incoming Wayne Pivac when he takes over as head coach in December.

An urgent item in his in-tray will be how to make Wales as effective in attack as they undoubtedly are in defence. Despite their Six Nations Grand Slam in 2019, they finished joint bottom, with Italy, in the try-scoring stakes. And whilst that might seem not seem to matter so long as the team are winning, there's a lingering sense that Wales will need to be more fruitful going forward if they're to trouble the world's best sides. But if the ex-outside half has any ideas about how to improve Welsh offensive play in future, he's not letting on today. Instead, with the Springboks on the horizon, it's all about basic principles:

"The key is: when we've got the ball, to be smart with it. It's about identifying where the space is, getting the ball to where that space is – on our terms – and enjoying having that ball."

"I thought [France] were particularly good in the first half [of the quarter-final]. They had the lion's share of possession and made it very difficult for us. But that's the nature of these games now: you're going to go through periods when you don't see the ball. You've just got to make sure you live in that fight and when you do get that ball, you make the most of it."

One man who's proved adept at making the most of his opportunities with ball in hand is George North. So much so that, at just 27, he's due to win his 90th cap tomorrow. A try against Georgia aside, North's been overshadowed in Japan by Josh Adams, his fellow winger. But tomorrow's opponents hold happy memories: he scored two tries on his debut against South Africa, aged 18.

"To get two tries on my debut was huge for me," George tells the media today. "It's been an amazing journey to get here. I've got an opportunity now to face South Africa again, but on a huge stage. And it's something I couldn't be more excited about."

Despite the fatigue from our late finish last night, a sense of that excitement is starting to filter through to us, too. One more win, and Wales are through to the World Cup Final, for the first time ever. This evening, they find out who they'll face if they get there. Tom, Siân and I head through the hustle and bustle of Shinjuku to our 'local', the Hub pub, to watch the first semi-final: New Zealand v. England. It's a mouth-watering prospect, with many making New Zealand favourites... but all week I've had a good feeling about England. They were imperious against Australia and, unlike Wales, they know how to beat the All Blacks.

There are few English fans in the pub, but a good smattering of Irish. Reluctantly, they're getting behind the men in white, perhaps because of their own humbling at the hands of the All Blacks. We're rooting for England too, unlike the Japanese drinkers, who are mostly New Zealand fans. For them, though, it's a disappointing evening, as England produce one of the great World Cup performances to shock the World Champions. From the moment they line up in arrow formation to face the haka, the English look totally up for it. Within 2 minutes they've scored, and, for most of the next 78, they dominate the New Zealanders in a way few ever have. The final scoreline of 19-7 actually flatters the All Blacks. England are through to the World Cup Final, and on this form, look nigh on unstoppable.

We head back for a nightcap in the hotel bar. Cigar smoke fills the air as fans of all nations discuss the evening's events and what's still ahead. Awesome though England were, Wales will know they've beaten them twice in 2019: it's an extra incentive, as if they needed one, to win against South Africa and reach the final.

The gauntlet has been thrown down: can Wales carry on where England left off? We're about to find out.

27 October: Wales v. South Africa

This job offers a few 'pinch me' moments, and today there's another one. When the three of us board the ITV Sport bus to the International Stadium in Yokohama, we join a veritable galaxy of stars. At the front there's Sir Clive Woodward, World Cup-winning coach from 2003. Further back we have Ben Kay, another World Cup-winner, and Paul O'Connell. My old pal Bryan Habana is here, and the trusty Welsh trio of Shane Williams, Gareth 'Alfie' Thomas and Mike Phillips. In rugby-playing circles, the back of the bus is apparently the domain of the oldest and most hardened: today, you'll find me, Tom and Siân sitting there, surveying the VIPs before us.

The weather's set fair and as we drive towards Yokohama – the place where Japan opened its doors to America and by extension, the West, back in 1854 – there's no chat about the game. Alfie wants to talk about today's South Wales football derby in Swansea; he, Mike and Shane natter amongst themselves, swapping stories. Habana, so I'm told by one of the ITV Sport staff, is more nervous about South Africa's prospects than he was yesterday, because of England's win. I suppose there's a certain logic at play: New Zealand beat South Africa, England beat New Zealand, Wales have beaten England recently, so Wales should beat South Africa, yes? If only life were so simple.

Whatever the outcome, it seems like a lot of people will be watching on TV. When we get to the ground, we're treated to a tour of the ITV pitchside studio by the Director of Photography, who happens to be from Penarth. It's a surprisingly small space, much smaller than it appears on TV, with a lot of very expensive gear inside. 11 million people tuned in for yesterday's England game, apparently; whatever the final figure is for today's match, it's a fair bet that lots of them will be watching from Wales.

How many of them would choose to watch another game like this is another matter, however. Everyone had expected lots of kicking from both teams tonight, and they're not disappointed. From the off, it's aerial ping-pong, with Gareth Davies and his opposite number Faf de Klerk taking it in turns to boot the ball high into the Yokohama sky. Meanwhile, two giant packs of forwards collide, each trying to impose themselves on the other.

Wales have the first half-chance, but a promising move down the left is called back for a forward pass. Five minutes later, they're penalised for not rolling away: Handré Pollard steps up to the tee, and South Africa are ahead.

Moments later, South Africa stray offside, and Biggar slots 3 points. But Wales aren't level for long. Under pressure, the scrum wheels, and Pollard kicks another goal: 3-6.

For 15 turgid minutes, not much happens. The teams battle for territory in the middle of the field, like two fighters slugging it out in the centre of the ring. Despite one mix-up with Gareth Davies, Halfpenny looks solid under the high ball, and the two packs seem to be cancelling each other out. But Wales are leaking more penalties, and eventually it tells: Ken Owens is offside at a maul, and Pollard extends the Springbok lead.

From the kick-off, Tomas Francis is injured, trying to make a tackle on Duane Vermeulen, and goes off. Then George North collapses in a heap while chasing a Biggar kick, and joins Francis on the sidelines. Biggar kicks the penalty to make it 6-9, but the injuries are mounting.

But as we know, Wales are nothing if not resilient. Five minutes after the start of the second half, they win a penalty and Biggar levels the scores. South Africa, suddenly, are looking shaky, spilling balls when before they'd looked secure. There's a bust-up, and Jake Ball squares up to de Klerk. But the Springboks are strong, too: suddenly, they're deep in Welsh territory. Pollard makes a half break, and when the ball comes back to Damian de Allende, the centre is strong enough to hold off the attentions of Biggar and Tomos Williams and score. Pollard converts: it's 19-16 to South Africa, and Wales are hanging on.

If ever, now's the time for a hero to step forward. Alun Wyn Jones, winning his 133rd cap tonight, is that man. With 16 minutes left, Wales win a penalty in front of the Springbok posts, and the Wales captain opts for a scrum. It's a brave move against South Africa, who are known for their scrummaging prowess, and who have six forward replacements on the bench. But gloriously, the gamble pays off. Moriarty frees the ball to Tomos Williams, Williams gives it to Jonathan Davies, and Davies puts Josh Adams over in the corner. What a moment to score your sixth World Cup try. With Biggar off, Halfpenny still has to slot the conversion from a narrow angle, but he does so: it's 16-16, with 14 minutes to play.

All of a sudden, the game roars into life. Wales have the ball again, inside the South African half, and they're battering away. Rhys Patchell is shaping for a drop goal, but he's too far out: if only Wales can get a bit closer. Eventually, they go for broke, but it's no good... Patchell's effort is unfortunately short and wide.

South Africa have weathered the storm. Can Wales? No. South Africa win a penalty, and kick for the corner. From the line-out, Wales are penalised again, and it's within kicking distance. Pollard – South Africa's leading points-scorer at World Cups – hasn't looked like missing all night, and doesn't. It's 16-19, with four minutes left.

Wales' World Cup is flashing before their eyes. They've got one more chance to stage a comeback, but this time, there's no resurrection. They concede another penalty, Pollard kicks the ball dead, and it's over.

"Congratulations to South Africa: they deserved to win," says Warren Gatland afterwards. "They were very good up front and defended exceptionally well. But I'm really proud of our guys. They never gave up, and got themselves back into the game."

For the players, the emotions are raw. Jonathan Davies has tears in his eyes, as do others. Under Gatland, Wales have now lost two semi-finals by a combined tally of 4 points. Asked by a post-match interviewer what it means to wear the red jersey, even Alun Wyn looks like choking up, before gathering himself.

"Hopefully I'll get another opportunity," he says. "It wasn't our day, but I'm still proud to pull this jersey on and represent all the people in red in the stadium."

"It was a one-score game, and they've probably taken their chances and we've left one or two out there," says Ken Owens, another senior player who may well be playing at his last World Cup. "But I think either side would have been disappointed to lose that – and we are, unfortunately."

"I can't question the effort and commitment of any of the players," says Josh Adams. "From 1-23 they put their bodies on the line and did what was asked of them. We played with our hearts on our sleeves tonight. We gave it everything we could, and we just came up short."

Several players say that they're determined to make the most of the next week, their last together as a squad, and to give Warren Gatland and the rest of the departing coaches a good send-off. A win over New Zealand in Friday's third-place play-off match would be a good way of doing that.

But whatever happens then, there's no disguising the hurt this evening. Emotionally exhausted, the three of us head back on the last ITV bus to Tokyo. This time, there are no ex-players on board.

After we've filed our report, we head down to the second floor, where a free bar soon rouses us from our despondency. I speak to Mike Phillips, who feels Wales could have played a bit more rugby, rather than being drawn into an arm-wrestle with South Africa. Former Scotland player Scott Hastings says he can appreciate what the players are going through, having experienced a World Cup semi-final defeat himself back in 1991. Miles Harrison, commentating for ITV during the World Cup, wonders if this is a sort of blessing in disguise: with their mounting injury list, Wales may not have been able to put their best foot forward against England next week.

When the dust has settled, there'll no doubt be an inquest. Maybe Wales could have gone wider against the Springboks; maybe the deficiencies in their attacking game have been exposed at last. But then it seems harsh to be too critical. As Gatland pointed out this week, Wales lack playing numbers compared with other countries. They do "punch above their weight". Gutting as tonight's result is, when you put it in those terms, to reach the last four – and come within a whisker of the last two – doesn't seem so bad after all.

11

Sayonara

In Japan, they have a concept known as *mono-no aware*. Literally, it means 'the pathos of things' and it's about the awareness that nothing lasts forever, and how that realisation is both sad and beautiful. Things may slip away, but at least you were there to witness them in the first place. It's why, each spring, Japanese people have picnics beneath the ubiquitous cherry blossom trees. They know that in the space of a few short weeks, the blossoms will fall to the ground. And somehow, that knowledge makes the experience all the sweeter.

It's the first week of November in Tokyo. Autumn is in the air, and everywhere you look, rugby eras are ending. Joe Schmidt, Jacques Brunel and Michael Cheika have already gone. Now, two even more garlanded coaches are following them into the sunset.

Neither Warren Gatland nor Steve Hansen were going to be judged on their last game in charge. After all, the third-place play-off (or 'bronze final', in the official parlance) is the game no one wants to play, and no one really remembers. And as we expected, it's a game too far for Wales: a patched-up team prove no match for the All Blacks, who score six tries in a 40-17 victory. At least Josh Adams has something to celebrate. His seventh tournament try sees him set a new record for tries by a Wales player at a World Cup.

Afterwards, Warren Gatland praises the Wales fans who have cheered the team on during his 12 years at the helm.

"I just want to say thank you to everyone back in Wales for the support I've had. I've loved my time in Wales – it's been a brilliant country to be a part of, and hopefully I'll be welcomed back at some stage!"

There's no sign of emotion. After all, as Gatland says, he's had a while to come to terms with the end of his tenure. Earlier in the week, he'd admitted to shedding a tear when walking off the Principality Stadium pitch following the summer's World Cup warm-up match against Ireland. And there's every chance he'll do the same at the end of November when he returns to Cardiff, this time as opposition coach, in charge of the Barbarians when they play Wales.

But there's no mistaking the New Zealander's sincerity when he talks about what Wales has meant to him, and how he hopes the success he enjoyed can continue under his countryman Wayne Pivac.

"I really hope – because of what we've achieved in the last 12 years, and because we feel like we've put some respect back into Wales as an international team – the new coaches come in and continue to build on that. After what we've done and achieved, it would break my heart if Wales went back into the doldrums."

"For such a small playing nation, we have to really push ourselves hard because we don't have the same number of players and depth of players. You've just got to wring the sponge as dry as you possibly can because that's the way we've performed and got results in the past."

He's certainly got results. Four Six Nations Championships, including three Grand Slams, a brief stint at number 1 in the world, and now a second World Cup semi-final – surely Gatland is the greatest Wales coach ever. And his successor will inherit a solid-looking squad. The average age of the team which took the field against New Zealand was 26, with only four players over 30. Looking at the squad as a whole, only a handful look like they'll be past it when France rolls around in four years' time. In the normal scheme of things, Alun Wyn Jones – who'll be a venerable 38 by then – would be one of them. But this is Alun Wyn we're talking about.

Wales will continue to face challenges, that much is certain. As of 2017, the country had 83,120 registered rugby players. As a proportion of the population (one player for every 36 people), that's not bad going: only the Pacific Islands and New Zealand have more, with Tonga leading the way with one player per 4.85 people. But in net terms, fewer people play the game in Wales than in any other top 8 nation. In England, there are 382,154 registered players. In France, it's a whopping 542,242. It's what Gatland was referring to when he talked about wringing the sponge dry. Without more people playing, Wales will continue to look short of depth when the inevitable injuries occur.

And improvements need to be made at the level below the international game. At time of writing, only one Welsh region (the Scarlets) was in the top half of its conference in the Guinness pro14, the domestic league. Over the last seven seasons, only one Welsh team has won the title. In Europe, the record is even more disappointing. In 25 years of trying, no Welsh club/region has ever won the main European competition. Only one has ever reached the final, and that was in 1996. And whilst the Blues deserve an honourable mention for twice lifting Europe's second tier trophy (rugby's equivalent, if you will, of soccer's Europa League), it's a record that compares poorly with that of the Irish provinces (seven Heineken or Champions' Cup wins), and English clubs (nine wins). That Gatland has achieved what he has with the national team is in spite, not because of, the infrastructure around it.

And as success breeds enthusiasm, so the opposite holds true: in the 2018/19 season, average crowds for the four Welsh regions were way below those of their rivals in the Guinness pro14. The Scarlets, with an average gate of 8,443, were the best attended, but the figure falls far below that for Leinster (17,242), and Munster and Ulster were also attracting audiences of more than 12,000. England's Aviva Premiership regularly draws crowds several times larger than those you'll find in Wales, while club rugby in France is also fervently supported. It's no wonder we have a problem holding onto players: faced with the prospect of playing in front of 14,000 every other week at, say, Bath, or fewer than half that number on a wet Friday night at Rodney Parade, which would you choose? For all the talk of tinkering with kick-off times, the old adage applies: nothing succeeds like success. When the regions are doing well, the fans are more likely to come and watch. The problem is, they're generally not.

At least the man about to take over the reins with Wales has shown he's able to break free of the mediocrity. Under Wayne Pivac, between 2016 and 2018 the Scarlets played some outstanding rugby, winning the Pro14 and reaching the Champions' Cup semi-final. Along the way, they wowed spectators with their fast and skilful style. Since then, things have regressed somewhat at Parc y Scarlets, it's true; but Pivac and his coaching team are clearly capable of inspiring their charges to great things.

"You only have to look at the way the Scarlets play and their recent achievements to get excited about the prospect of Wayne Pivac coaching Wales," said WRU Chairman Gareth Davies back in 2018, when Pivac was unveiled as Warren Gatland's successor. "We have undertaken a hugely thorough process to make this appointment. It has been more than two years in the making and we were both impressed by Wayne throughout, and by the variety of his accomplishments during a lengthy career in coaching."

In Gatland, Pivac undoubtedly has a tough act to follow. But New Zealand coaches tend to do well in Wales (think Graham Henry and Steve Hansen [after his shaky start] as well as Warren), and the new man's had plenty of time to ponder his strategy. Let's hope he's given time to implement his ideas, and that his illustrious predecessor doesn't cast too long a shadow.

So much for Wales. But what shape is world rugby in, as its quadrennial jamboree draws to a close? In many ways, the answer seems to be: in rude health. According to the organisers, matches in Japan were the best attended ever, with 99.3% of the seats filled over the 45 matches. A record 1.13 million people visited the fanzones. Perhaps the boldest claim relates to the legacy of the tournament: World Rugby reckons that 1.8 million more youngsters are playing rugby in Asia as a result of the World Cup. If this is true, the sporting landscape in Japan and surrounding countries really could be changing. The home nation undoubtedly played the tournament's most exciting rugby in 2019, so if this new generation of youngsters continues to play the game, who knows what it might achieve in future.

There's been speculation about the Brave Blossoms joining the Rugby Championship, or even the Six Nations. You also wonder where the authorities might look to stage future World Cups, given the success of the 2019 edition. In his final press conference of the tournament, Warren Gatland suggested that the USA might be a good destination. Surely, if World Rugby are serious in their stated aim of spreading the gospel beyond the game's traditional bastions, it's an option they should consider.

2019 will also be remembered for the governing body's new 'high tackle framework', with its emphasis on player welfare. At the tournament, a record eight red cards were handed out – twice as many as in 1995 and 1999, where there were four dismissals each time – while players who escaped on-field punishment, such as Australia's Reece Hodge, were later handed significant bans. Most had made tackles which, in previous years, would have attracted a penalty at most. Some former players have attacked the new guidelines, saying the game is in danger of becoming 'soft'. Others say the impetus to lower tackle heights and protect players' heads is something that is long overdue.

Having sat through several interludes where play was held up so officials could review a tackle, I can understand the frustration of spectators. I also think it's asking a lot of players to always get their tackle technique right in a game with so many variables, and where decisions are made at lightning speed. But, in the end, it's hard to argue with anything which safeguards peoples' health, and saves them from the unpleasant consequences of concussion in later life. Interestingly, towards the end of the tournament, World Rugby released figures suggesting concussion rates are indeed down as a result of the changes.

The day after Wales' bronze-final game, South Africa upset the odds to beat England 32-12 and lift the Webb Ellis Cup, equalling the All Blacks' record of three wins since the tournament's inception. For us, meanwhile, it's almost time to go home. And it feels like as good a time as any to reflect on our great adventure.

My personal memories of the tournament, the first to be held in Japan? Well, I guess I have to start with the hospitality and warmth of the Japanese people. Chatting last week, the three of us realised a strange thing: only once since we'd been here had we heard the sound of a car horn being honked. That's seven and a half weeks, including three in the world's biggest and busiest city. And that one time, it was a westerner behind the wheel. The Japanese seem to have almost supernatural powers of patience and courtesy. It's vanishingly rare to see a Japanese person wound up or annoyed. And that's a lovely thing, even if they can sometimes seem a little over-bound by their rules and regulations. Then there's the kindness: the stranger in Tokyo who paid our bar bill, the shopworker who ran halfway across Kumamoto Station to give me back the piece of kit I'd dropped, the three folk from the Tokyo Skytree who lit up Japan's tallest building in red, just for us. You can't quite believe you're being treated so well.

And what pride. Hours after the country was hit by its worst typhoon in 60 years, the staff at Yokohama Stadium were working away, trying to get the arena ready for a crucial game. Despite the grief, the shock, nothing would stop them from doing what they'd set out to do.

As a journalist, it's glib to describe things as unforgettable. But I can honestly say that seeing 15,000 people in a remote corner of Japan singing 'Calon Lân' and 'Hen Wlad Fy Nhadau' on a Monday afternoon is a sight I'll remember till my dying day. Not just the fact they turned up, but the sheer fervour they put into learning the songs and cheering the players... in a cynical world, what a delightful lack of cynicism.

Who knows what the future holds for Wales? Who knows if they can ever win a World Cup? But whatever happens, whatever ups and downs the game throws at them, Japan 2019 has taught them – and all of us – a great lesson. What happens on the pitch is the least important thing. Sporting dynasties bloom and wilt like blossoms on the cherry tree. It's the values that endure: the brotherhood, the inspiration, the fellowship, the love. All the things that stay true in this impermanent world.

By the same author:

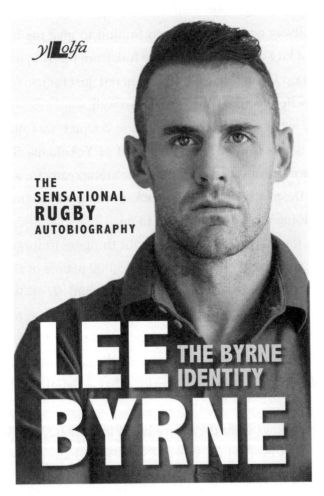

y Lolfa

THE
SENSATIONAL
RUGBY
AUTOBIOGRAPHY

LEE THE BYRNE IDENTITY
BYRNE

£9.99

Also from Y Lolfa:

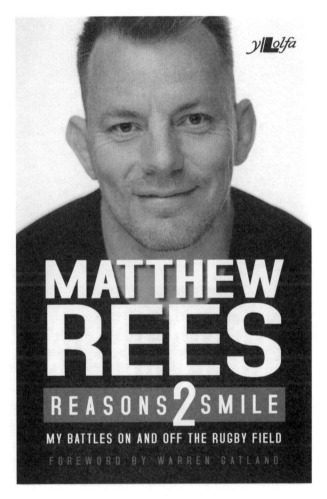

£9.99

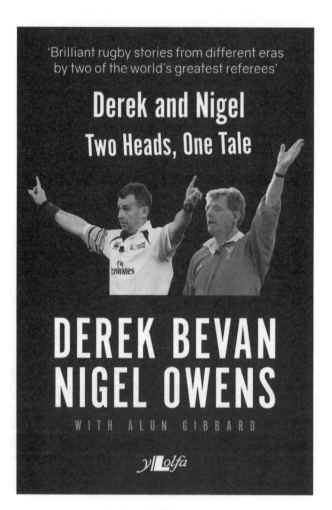

'Brilliant rugby stories from different eras by two of the world's greatest referees'

Derek and Nigel
Two Heads, One Tale

DEREK BEVAN
NIGEL OWENS

WITH ALUN GIBBARD

y Lolfa

£7.99

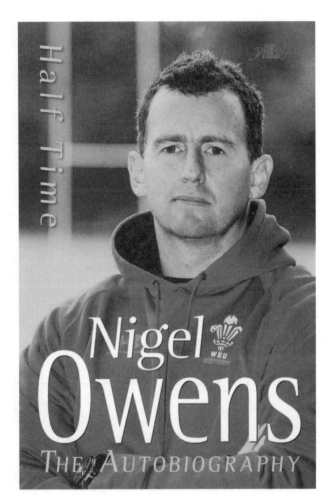

Half Time

Nigel
Owens

The Autobiography

£9.95

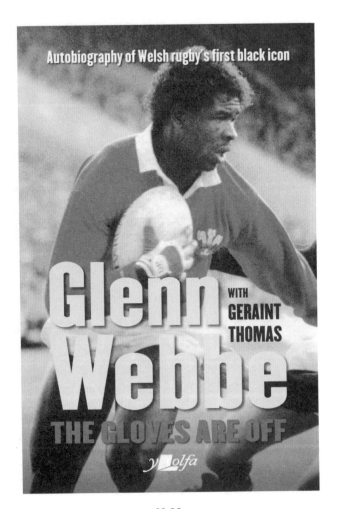

Autobiography of Welsh rugby's first black icon

Glenn Webbe

WITH GERAINT THOMAS

THE GLOVES ARE OFF

y Lolfa

£9.99

LYNN DAVIES

hard men
of WELSH
RUGBY

yl Lolfa

£7.95